Born on a Blue Day

A Memoir of Asperger's and an Extraordinary Mind

Daniel Tammet

HODDER

Copyright © 2006 by Daniel Tammet

First published in Great Britain in 2006 by Hodder & Stoughton
A division of Hodder Headline

This edition first published in 2007

The right of Daniel Tammet to be identified as the Author
of the Work has been asserted by him in accordance with
the Copyright, Designs and Patents Act 1988.

A Hodder & Stoughton book

19

A CIP catalogue record for this title is available from the British Library

ISBN 978 0 340 89975 5

Typeset in Plantin Light by Hewer Text UK Ltd, Edinburgh
Printed and bound by Clays Ltd, St Ives plc

Hodder Headline's policy is to use papers that are natural, renewable
and recyclable products and made from wood grown in sustainable forests.
The logging and manufacturing processes are expected to conform to
the environmental regulations of the country of origin.

Hodder & Stoughton Ltd
A division of Hodder Headline
338 Euston Road
London NW1 3BH

To my parents,
for helping me become the person I am today
and to Neil,
for always being there for me

Acknowledgements

I would like to thank the following people, without whom this book would never have been possible:

My parents, Jennifer and Kevin, for all their love and patience and for all that they have taught me

My brothers Lee, Steven and Paul and sisters Claire, Maria, Natasha, Anna-Marie and Shelley, for their love and understanding

Rehan Qayoom – my best friend from my schooldays

Elfriede Corkhill – my favourite schoolteacher

Ian and Elaine Moore, Ian and Ana Williams and Olly and Ash Jeffery – my closest friends

Birutė Ziliene – the person I think of when I remember my time in Lithuania

Sigriður Kristinsdóttir – my Icelandic tutor

Suzy Seraphine-Kimel and Julien Chaumon – for all their help with the Optimnem.co.uk website

Martin, Steve, Toby, Dan and Nicola – the team behind the *Brainman* documentary

Andrew Lownie, my literary agent; Rowena Webb, Helen Coyle and Kerry Hood at Hodder for all their help and advice with the book

Finally my partner Neil, for being himself

Contents

Foreword by Dr Darold Treffert

This is a concise book about a very expansive mind. But it is a book not just about the *mind* of Daniel Tammet, but a book about his *world* as well. And both are worthy of exploration.

Daniel's phenomenal ability with numbers is incredible. If you ask him to multiply 37 to the power of 4 he will give you almost instantly the total of 1,874,161. Ask him to divide 13 by 97 and he will give you the answer to over 100 decimal places if you wish. He outdistances the ordinary calculator instantly and without effort. You'll need a computer to see if he is correct. And of course he is correct. Then there is his ability to learn an entire new language – grammar, inflection and comprehension in only one week. The documentary Brainman, first broadcast in the U.K. in 2005, charts Daniel's mastery of Icelandic in such a brief time, culminating in a live interview on television using his newly acquired language in a sprightly interaction with his Icelandic TV hosts.

Of special interest for me, though, is not just what Daniel can so extraordinarily do, but rather his capacity to describe how he does it. Such first-person explanations of savant abilities are extremely rare, in fact nearly non-existent. Most books are written by others about the special abilities some people have, rather than having been written by the person who has those special skills. Daniel, uniquely, provides an exceptionally insightful account of his mental capacities. This description can now be correlated with imaging studies and other neuropsychological tests, some already underway, thereby providing a rare opportunity to explore more fully the elusive, "how do they do it?" question.

But other things are of interest as well. Daniel's synaesthesia, which he describes so richly, is unique in that he 'sees' individual numbers – each one up to 10,000 – not just as a single colour, but also as a shape, a colour, a texture, a motion and sometimes even an emotional 'tone'. When he does his massive calculations he literally 'sees' the answer in his head, not written out in number form as in a telephone book, but rather as a confluence of these shapes and colours and forms into an 'answer' experienced in a newly coalesced shape, form and colour.

Daniel tells us that his synaesthesia began after a series of childhood epileptic seizures. This, for me, puts him into the "acquired" savant category – people who develop savant-like abilities, sometimes at a prodigious level, following some central nervous system trauma, disease or disorder. The "acquired" savant raises important questions about hidden potential, perhaps, dormant within us all, and about how to tap that potential without traumatic event. By studying Daniel more closely – something he is very willing to participate in – we may come closer to being able to tap the "little Rainman" that exists, perhaps, within us all.

Daniel has also been given a diagnosis of high functioning autism, or Asperger's Disorder as well, a condition he writes openly about. In contrast to the more prominent symptoms and behaviours he displayed as a child, though, his present very high level of functioning underscores his observation that he has "outgrown" some of his autism. Such progress does occur, fortunately, in some other people on the autistic spectrum, as they grow older. Daniel's part progress has created in him a heartfelt life mission – to serve as an inspiration for other people, whether with epilepsy or Asperger's, demonstrating by his own example that such conditions need not always interfere with overall development and potential. His mission statement is an empathic one – to make the world a "more welcome place" for people with such disabilities.

I met Daniel for the first time at the Milwaukee Art Museum with its dramatic architecture, rich colours and striking imagery. It was the perfect setting. A towering sculpture with a multitude of glass pieces, of all shapes, sizes and colours, helped me visualise, in a concrete sense, some of the vivid thought imagery that Daniel was describing to me verbally.

In person Daniel is articulate, soft-spoken, pleasant, polite, gentle and modest. Those traits shine through in his writing as well. His plans for the future include continuing to help charities such as the National Autistic Society and the National Society for Epilepsy. His celebrity-status gives him a good podium world-wide from which to carry out that admirable goal. He also wants to continue to work with scientists to study his special abilities in greater detail. And he wants to promote different ways of learning, particularly visual learning, which is so often so important in better understanding, and then teaching, people with autistic spectrum disorders.

At a very personal level his goals mirror those of most of us – becoming closer in our relationships with partners, family and friends. He also wants to seek, and relish, those too few, but precious moments of peace and contentment that he describes in the closing para-graphs of his book. Those are 'heavenly' moments.

Daniel says that numbers are his friends. Indeed in his early childhood they seemed to be his only friends. But now Daniel is seeking out and making new friends – literally all over the world. Friendship is reciprocal though. And one comes away from his book – or at least I did – with the feeling, through his openness, candor and reaching out, of having made a new friend as well.

Darold A. Treffert, M.D.
Scientific adviser on the film *Rainman*

Foreword by
Professor Simon Baron-Cohen

"How rare is it to have synaesthesia? It occurs in less than 1% of the population. And how rare is it to have an autism spectrum condition? Again, less than 1% of the population has such a condition. In Daniel Tammet, these two states co-occur and if we assume they are independent, the probability of someone having both synaesthesia and autism is vanishingly small – about 1 in 10,000. In this, his first book, Daniel tells 'with engaging detail' the story of his life, from his childhood when he always felt he was an outsider, to his adulthood, when among many other extraordinary achievements, he sets a British and European record for reciting the mathematical constant Pi from memory, to 22,514 decimal places. His other gifts include acquiring foreign languages with ease, and even having constructed his own language. Are his talents the result of his two rare syndromes coming together in one person? His synaesthesia gives him a richly textured, multi-sensory form of memory, and his autism gives him the narrow focus on number and syntactic patterns. The resulting book is a story of a life that is both remarkable and inspiring."

Simon Baron-Cohen
Director, Autism Research Centre
Cambridge University

1

Blue Nines and Red Words

I was born on 31 January 1979 – a Wednesday. I know it was a Wednesday, because the date is blue in my mind and Wednesdays are always blue, like the number nine or the sound of loud voices arguing. I like my birth date, because of the way I'm able to visualise most of the numbers in it as smooth and round shapes, similar to pebbles on a beach. That's because they are prime numbers: 31, 19, 197, 97, 79 and 1979 are all divisible only by themselves and one. I can recognise every prime up to 9973 by their 'pebble-like' quality. It's just the way my brain works.

I have a rare condition known as savant syndrome,

little known before its portrayal by actor Dustin Hoffman in the Oscar-winning 1988 film *Rain Man*. Like Hoffman's character, Raymond Babbitt, I have an almost obsessive need for order and routine, which affects virtually every aspect of my life. For example, I eat exactly 45 grams of porridge for breakfast each morning; I weigh the bowl with an electronic scale to make sure. Then I count the number of items of clothing I'm wearing before I leave my house. I get anxious if I can't drink my cups of tea at the same time each day. Whenever I become too stressed and I can't breathe properly, I close my eyes and count. Thinking of numbers helps me to become calm again.

Numbers are my friends and they are always around me. Each one is unique and has its own personality. Eleven is friendly and five is loud, whereas four is both shy and quiet – it's my favourite number, perhaps because it reminds me of myself. Some are big – 23, 667, 1179 – while others are small: 6, 13, 581. Some are beautiful, like 333, and some are ugly, like 289. To me, every number is special.

No matter where I go or what I'm doing, numbers are never far from my thoughts. In an interview with chat show host David Letterman in New York, I told David he looked like the number 117 – tall and lanky. Later outside, in the appropriately numerically named Times Square, I gazed up at the towering skyscrapers and felt surrounded by nines – the number I most associate with feelings of immensity.

Scientists call my visual, emotional experience of numbers synaesthesia, a rare neurological mixing of the senses, which most commonly results in the ability to see alphabetical letters and/or numbers in colour. Mine is an unusual and complex type, through which I see numbers as shapes, colours, textures and motions. The number one, for example, is a brilliant and bright white, like someone shining a torch beam into my eyes. Five is a clap of thunder or the sound of waves crashing against rocks. Thirty-seven is lumpy like porridge, while eighty-nine reminds me of falling snow.

37   89

Probably the most famous case of synaesthesia was the one written up over a period of thirty years from the 1920s by the Russian psychologist A.R. Luria of a journalist called Shereshevsky who had a prodigious memory. 'S', as Luria called him in his notes for the book *The Mind of a Mnemonist*, had a highly visual memory which allowed him to 'see' words and numbers as different shapes and colours. 'S' was able to remember a matrix of 50 digits after studying it for three minutes, both immediately afterwards and many years later. Luria credited Shereshevsky's synaesthetic experiences as the basis for his remarkable short- and long-term memory.

Using my own synaesthetic experiences since early childhood, I have grown up with the ability to handle and calculate huge numbers in my head without any conscious effort, just like the Raymond Babbitt character. In fact, this is a talent common to several other real-life savants (sometimes referred to as 'lightning calculators'). Dr Darold Treffert, a Wisconsin physician and the leading researcher in the study of savant syndrome, gives one example, of a blind man with 'a faculty of calculating to a degree little short of marvellous' in his book *Extraordinary People*:

> When he was asked how many grains of corn there would be in any one of 64 boxes, with 1 in the first, 2 in the second, 4 in the third, 8 in the fourth, and so on, he gave answers for the fourteenth (8,192), for the eighteenth (131,072) and the twenty-fourth (8,388,608) instantaneously, and he gave the figures for the forty-eighth box (140,737,488,355,328) in six seconds. He also gave the total in all 64 boxes correctly (18,446,744,073,709,551,616) in forty-five seconds.

My favourite kind of calculation is power multiplication, which means multiplying a number by itself a specified number of times. Multiplying a number by itself is called squaring; for example, the square of 72 is $72 \times 72 = 5,184$. Squares are always symmetrical shapes in my mind, which makes them especially beautiful to me. Multiplying the same number three times over is called cubing or 'raising' to the third power. The cube or third power of 51 is equivalent to $51 \times 51 \times 51 = 132,651$. I see each result of a power multiplication as a distinctive visual pattern in my head. As the sums and their results grow, so the mental shapes and colours I experience become increasingly more complex. I see thirty-seven's fifth power – $37 \times 37 \times 37 \times 37 \times 37 = 69,343,957$ – as a large circle composed of smaller circles running clockwise from the top round.

When I divide one number by another, in my head I see a spiral rotating downwards in larger and larger loops, which seem to warp and curve. Different divisions produce different sizes of spirals with varying curves. From my mental imagery I'm able to calculate a sum like $13 \div 97$ (0.1340206 . . .) to almost a hundred decimal places.

I never write anything down when I'm calculating, because I've always been able to do the sums in my head and it's much easier for me to visualise the answer using my synaesthetic shapes than to try to follow the 'carry the one' techniques taught in the textbooks we are given at school. When multiplying, I see the two numbers as distinct shapes. The image changes and a third shape emerges – the correct answer. The process takes a matter of seconds and happens spontaneously. It's like doing maths without having to think.

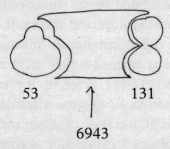

53   ↑   131

6943

In the illustration above I'm multiplying 53 by 131. I see both numbers as a unique shape and locate each spatially opposite the other. The space created between the two shapes creates a third, which I perceive as a new number: 6,943, the solution to the sum.

Different tasks involve different shapes and I also have various sensations or emotions for certain numbers. Whenever I multiply with eleven I always experience a feeling of the digits tumbling downwards in my head. I find sixes hardest to remember of all the numbers, because I experience them as tiny black dots, without any distinctive shape or texture. I would describe them as like little gaps or holes. I have visual and sometimes emotional responses to every number up to 10,000, like having my own visual, numerical vocabulary. And just like a poet's choice of words, I find some combinations of numbers more beautiful than others: ones go well with darker numbers like eights and nines, but not so well with sixes. A telephone number with the sequence 189 is much more beautiful to me than one with a sequence like 116.

This aesthetic dimension to my synaesthesia is something that has its ups and downs. If I see a number I experience as particularly beautiful on a shop sign or a car number plate, there's a shiver of excitement and pleasure. On the other hand, if the numbers don't match my experience of them, if for example a shop sign's price has '99p' in red or green (instead of blue), then I find that uncomfortable and irritating.

It is not known how many savants have synaesthetic experiences to help them in the areas they excel in. One reason for this is that, like Raymond Babbitt, many suffer profound mental and/or physical disability, preventing them from explaining to others how they do the things that they do. I am fortunate not to suffer from any of the most severe impairments that often come with abilities such as mine.

Like most individuals with savant syndrome, I am also on the autistic spectrum. I have Asperger's syndrome, a relatively mild and high-functioning form of autism that affects around 1 in every 300 people in the UK. According to a 2001 study by the UK's National Autistic Society, nearly half of all adults with Asperger's syndrome are not diagnosed until after the age of sixteen. I was finally diagnosed at age twenty-five following tests and an interview at the Autism Research Centre in Cambridge.

Autism, including Asperger's syndrome, is defined

by the presence of impairments affecting social inter-action, communication and imagination (problems with abstract or flexible thought and empathy, for example). Diagnosis is not easy and cannot be made by a blood test or brain scan; doctors have to observe behaviour and study the individual's developmental history from infancy.

People with Asperger's often have good language skills and are able to lead relatively normal lives. Many have above-average IQs and excel in areas that involve logical or visual thinking. Like other forms of autism, Asperger's is a condition affecting many more men than women (around 80% of autistics and 90% of those diagnosed with Asperger's are men). Single-minded-ness is a defining characteristic, as is a strong drive to analyse detail and identify rules and patterns in sys-tems. Specialised skills involving memory, numbers and mathematics are common. It is not known for certain what causes someone to have Asperger's, though it is something you are born with.

For as long as I can remember, I have experienced numbers in the visual, synaesthetic way that I do. Numbers are my first language, one I often think and feel in. Emotions can be hard for me to understand or know how to react to, so I often use numbers to help me. If a friend says they feel sad or depressed, I picture myself sitting in the dark hollowness of number six to help me experience the same sort of feeling and understand it. If I read in an article that a person felt intimidated by something, I imagine myself standing next to the number nine. Whenever someone describes visiting a beautiful place, I recall my numerical landscapes and how happy they make me feel inside. By doing this, numbers actually help me get closer to understanding other people.

Sometimes people I meet for the first time remind me of a particular number and this helps me to be comfortable around them. They might be very tall and remind me of the number nine, or round and remind me of the number three. If I feel unhappy or anxious or in a situation I have no previous experience of (when I'm much more likely to feel stressed and uncomfortable), I count to myself. When I count, the numbers form pictures and patterns in my mind that are consistent and reassuring to me. Then I can relax and interact with whatever situation I'm in.

Thinking of calendars always makes me feel good, all those numbers and patterns in one place. Different days of the week elicit different colours and emotions in my head: Tuesdays are a warm colour while Thursdays are fuzzy. Calendrical calculation – the ability to tell what day of the week a particular date fell or will fall on – is common to many savants. I think this is probably due to the fact that the numbers in calendars are predictable and form patterns between the different days and months. For example, the thirteenth day in a month is always two days before whatever day the first

falls on, while several of the months mimic the behaviour of others, like January and October, September
and December and February and March (the first day
of January is the same as the first day of October). So if
the first of January is a fuzzy texture in my mind
(Thursday) for a given year, the thirteenth of October
will be a warm colour (Tuesday).

In his book *The Man Who Mistook His Wife for a Hat*,
writer and neurologist Oliver Sacks mentions the case
of severely autistic twins John and Michael as an
example of how far some savants are able to take
calendrical calculations. Though unable to care for
themselves (they had been in various institutions since
the age of seven), the twins were capable of calculating
the day of the week for any date over a 40,000-year
span.

Sacks also describes John and Michael playing a
game for hours at a time that involved swapping prime
numbers with each other. Like the twins, I have always
been fascinated by prime numbers. I see each prime as
a smooth textured shape, distinct from composite
numbers (non-primes) that are grittier and less distinctive. Whenever I identify a number as prime, I get a
rush of feeling in my head (in the front centre) which is
hard to put into words. It's a special feeling, like the
sudden sensation of pins and needles.

Sometimes I close my eyes and imagine the first
thirty, fifty, hundred numbers as I experience them
spatially, synaesthetically. Then I can see in my mind's

eye just how beautiful and special the primes are by the way they stand out so sharply from the other number shapes. It's exactly for this reason that I look and look and look at them; each one is so different from the one before and the one after. Their loneliness among the other numbers makes them so conspicuous and interesting to me.

There are moments, as I'm falling into sleep at night, that my mind fills suddenly with bright light and all I can see are numbers – hundreds, thousands of them – swimming rapidly over my eyes. The experience is beautiful and soothing to me. Some nights, when I'm having difficulty falling asleep, I imagine myself walking around my numerical landscapes. Then I feel safe and happy. I never feel lost, because the prime number shapes act as signposts.

Mathematicians, too, spend a lot of time thinking about prime numbers, in part because there is no quick or simple method for testing a number to see whether or not it is prime. The best known is called 'The Sieve of Eratosthenes' after an ancient Greek scholar, Eratosthenes of Cyrene. The sieve method works in this way: Write out the numbers you want to test, for example 1–100. Starting with 2 (1 is neither prime nor composite), cross out every second number: 4, 6, 8 . . . up to 100. Then move to 3 and cross out every third number: 6, 9, 12 . . . then move to 5 and cross out every fifth number: 10, 15, 20 . . . and so on, until you are left with only a few numbers that do not ever get

crossed out: 2, 3, 5, 7, 11, 13, 17, 19, 23, 29, 31 . . .
These are the prime numbers; the building blocks of
my numerical world.

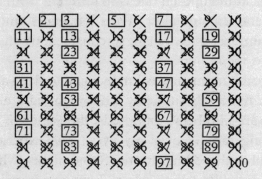

My synaesthesia also affects how I perceive words and
language. The word 'ladder', for example, is blue and
shiny, while 'hoop' is a soft, white word. The same
thing happens when I read words in other languages:
jardin, the French word for garden, is a blurred yellow
while *hnugginn* – Icelandic for 'sad' – is white with lots
of blue specks. Synaesthesia researchers have reported
that coloured words tend to obtain their colours from
the initial letter of the word, and this is generally true
for me: 'yoghurt' is a yellow word, 'video' is purple
(perhaps linked with 'violet') and 'gate' is green. I can
even make the colour of a word change by mentally
adding initial letters to turn the word into another: 'at'
is a red word, but add the letter H to get 'hat' and it
becomes a white word. If I then add a letter T to make
'that', the word's colour is now orange. Not all words

fit the initial letter pattern: words beginning with the letter A, for example, are always red and those beginning with W are always dark blue.

Some words are perfect fits for the things they describe. A raspberry is both a red word and a red fruit, while 'grass' and 'glass' are both green words that describe green things. Words beginning with the letter T are always orange like a tulip or a tiger or a tree in autumn, when the leaves turn to orange.

Conversely, some words do not seem to me to fit the things they describe: 'geese' is a green word, but describes white birds ('heese' would seem a better choice to me), the word 'white' is blue while 'orange' is clear and shiny like ice. 'Four' is a blue word but a pointy number, at least to me. The colour of wine (a blue word) is better described by the French word *vin*, which is purple.

Seeing words in different colours and textures aids my memory for facts and names. For example, I remember that the winning cyclist of each stage of the Tour de France wins a yellow jersey (not green or red or blue), because the word 'jersey' is yellow to me. Similarly, I can remember that Finland's national flag has a blue cross (on a white background) because the word 'Finland' is blue (as are all words beginning with the letter F). When I meet someone for the first time I often remember their name by the colour of the word: Richards are red, Johns are yellow and Henrys are white.

It also helps me to learn other languages quickly and easily. I currently know ten languages: English (my native language), Finnish, French, German, Lithuanian, Esperanto, Spanish, Romanian, Icelandic and Welsh. Associating the different colours and emotions I experience for each word with its meaning helps bring the words to life. For example, the Finnish word *tuli* is orange to me and means 'fire'. When I read or think about the word I immediately see the colour in my head, which evokes the meaning. Another example is the Welsh word *gweilgi*, which is a green and dark blue colour and means 'sea'. I think it is an extremely good word for describing the sea's colours. Then there is the Icelandic word *rökkur*, which means 'twilight' or 'dusk'. It is a crimson word and when I see it, it makes me think of a blood-red sunset.

I remember as a young child, during one of my frequent trips to the local library, spending hours looking at book after book trying in vain to find one that had my name on it. Because there were so many books in the library, with so many different names on them, I'd assumed that one of them – somewhere – had to be mine. I didn't understand at the time that a person's name appears on a book because he or she wrote it. Now that I'm twenty-six I know better. If I were ever going to find my book one day, I was going to have to write it first.

Writing about my life has given me the opportunity

to get some perspective on just how far I've come, and to trace the arc of my journey up to the present. If someone had told my parents ten years ago that I would be living completely independently, with a loving relationship and a career, I don't think they would have believed it and I'm not sure I would have done either. This book will tell you how I got there.

My younger brother Steven has recently been diagnosed with the same form of high-functioning autism that I have. At nineteen, he is going through a lot of the challenges that I too faced while growing up, from problems with anxiety and loneliness to uncertainty about the future. When I was a child, doctors did not know about Asperger's syndrome (it was not recognised as a unique disorder until 1994) and so for many years I grew up with no understanding of why I felt so different from my peers and apart from the world around me. By writing about my own experiences of growing up on the autistic spectrum, it is my hope that I can help other young people living with high-functioning autism, like my brother Steven, to feel less isolated and to have confidence in the knowledge that it is ultimately possible to lead a happy and productive life. I'm living proof of that.

2

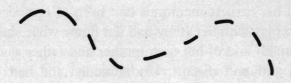

Early Years

It was a bitterly cold January morning in East London. My mother, Jennifer by then heavily pregnant with me, was sitting and gazing out silently from the only large window in the flat over the narrow, frozen street below. My father, Kevin a habitual early riser, was surprised to find her awake as he walked in with the day's paper from the local shop. Worried that something might be wrong, he quietly approached and held her hand. She seemed tired, as she had for the past several weeks, and remained motionless, her gaze fixed and silent. Then slowly she turned to him, her face etched with emotion as her hands hovered gently over her stomach, and said: 'Whatever happens, we'll love him, just love him.' My mother began to cry and my father squeezed her hand in his and nodded silently.

She had always considered herself an outsider as a child; her earliest memories had been of brothers too old to play with her (they had left home while she was still small) and of her own mother and father as quite often stiff and distant. Undoubtedly, she had been loved, but had rarely felt it growing up. Her childhood recollections continued to bristle with emotional ambiguity even thirty years later.

My father had been devoted to my mother from the time he had first met her, through mutual friends, and following a whirlwind romance they had made a home together. He had little to offer her, so he had thought, but his devotion.

As a child, he had brought up his younger brothers and sisters single-handedly while his mother, divorced from my grandfather, worked away from home for long periods at a time. At the age of ten, my father had taken it upon himself to look after them when the family moved into a hostel for the homeless. There had been little time for school or for the usual hopes and dreams of childhood. He would later recall the day he met my mother as the happiest of his life. Though very different people, they had made the other feel special and, for all the difficulties in their own upbringings, they had wanted nothing less than the same for me.

Days after their emotional conversation, my mother

went into labour. Arriving home from work that evening, my father found her wracked with pain. She had waited for him, afraid to go to the hospital without him. He phoned for an ambulance and, his clothes still caked in oil and grease from his sheet metal work, he rushed with my mother to the hospital. The delivery was swift and I came into the world weighing just under six pounds.

It is said that the arrival of a baby changes everything, and my birth certainly changed my parents' lives forever. I was their first child, so it is perhaps natural that they had invested so much of their hope for the future in me, even before I was born. My mother had spent the months leading up to my birth eagerly combing the advice columns of popular women's magazines for baby care tips and together with my father had saved specially for a cot.

Yet my mother's first days with me at the hospital were not as she had imagined them. I cried constantly for hours at a time. It didn't seem to matter that she held me close to her, stroking my face gently with her fingers; I cried and cried and cried.

The flat where my parents lived was small and I was to sleep in a cot in the corner of their single bedroom. After my arrival from the hospital my parents found it impossible to lay me inside it; I would not sleep and I continued to cry incessantly. I was breastfed for the next eighteen months; not least because it was one of the very few methods my mother found to help quieten me.

Breastfeeding has long been known to be good for babies, helping to enhance cognitive development and sensory skills as well as the baby's immune system. It is also thought to be beneficial to the emotional development of children on the autistic spectrum, providing a special opportunity for close physical and emotional contact between mother and child. Research indicates that autistic children who were breastfed are more responsive, socially adjusted and affectionate than their formula-fed peers.

Another means my parents found to relieve my crying was to give me the sensation of motion. My father regularly rocked me in his arms, sometimes for more than an hour at a time. It was not uncommon for him to have to eat his meals with one hand and hold and rock me with his other arm. He also took me in a pram for long walks in the street after work, often in the early hours of the morning. The moment the pram came to a stop I began to bawl again.

It soon didn't matter whether it was day or night, as my parents' lives quickly began to revolve around my crying. I must have driven them to distraction. In their despair they often put me in a blanket, my mother holding one end and my father the other, and swung me from side to side. The repetition seemed to soothe me.

That summer, I was christened. Even though my parents weren't churchgoers themselves, I was their firstborn and they thought it was the right thing to do.

All manner of relatives, friends and neighbours attended and the weather was warm and clear. But come the service I cried and cried, drowning out the words spoken during the ceremony. My parents were deeply embarrassed.

My mother's parents visited us and wondered why it was that I was such a difficult baby. They suggested that my mother not pick me up when I began crying. 'He'll soon wear himself out,' they said. But when my mother followed this advice my crying just became louder and louder.

My parents called the doctor out on many occasions, but each time he would say I was suffering from colic and that I would get better soon. Colic is often referred to as 'unexplained crying', where the baby cries longer and louder than average and is harder to console. About one in five babies cry enough to meet the definition of colic. Doctors and scientists have been trying for decades to find the cause behind these babies' excessive crying. The most recent idea is that most forms of colic are developmental and neurological, arising from the brain, rather than – as many parents assume – the baby's digestive system. For instance, colicky babies tend to be unusually sensitive to stimulation and are likely to be vulnerable to sensory overload.

The duration of my excessive crying – lasting well into my first year – is unusual, even for colicky babies. Recently, researchers studying the development of children with a history of prolonged crying in baby-hood found that it may be a sign of future behavioural problems. Compared to children who cried normally as babies, at age five, children who had cried exces-sively were found to have poorer hand-eye coordina-tion and to be prone to hyperactivity or present discipline problems.

Fortunately, my development was fine in other areas: I was walking and saying my first words not long after my first birthday. One of the criteria for a diagnosis of Asperger's is the absence of any significant delay in language (as opposed to more severe forms of autism where language can be considerably delayed or even non-existent).

There followed a series of recurring ear infections, for which I was given antibiotics. Because of the pain caused by the infections, I remained a cranky, sickly and crying child well into my second year. Throughout all this time my parents, though frequently exhausted by me, continued to swing me in the blanket and rock me in their arms every day.

And then, amidst the constant crying and illness, my mother discovered she was pregnant. My parents applied to the local council for a larger home and we subsequently moved to a flat close by. Lee, my brother, was born on a Sunday in May and he was the complete opposite to me: happy, calm and quiet. It must have been an immense relief to my parents.

My behaviour, however, did not improve. At age two

I began to walk up to a particular wall in the living room and bang my head against it. I would rock my body backwards and forwards, striking my forehead hard, repeatedly and rhythmically, against the wall. Sometimes I would bang my head with such force that I got bruises. My father would pull me away from the wall whenever he heard the familiar banging sound, but I'd run back and start all over again. At other times I went into violent tantrums, slapping my head over and over with my hand and screaming at the top of my voice.

My parents called in the health visitor. She reassured them that head banging was a child's way of soothing himself when he feels some kind of distress. She suggested that I was frustrated and under-stimulated and promised to help find a place for me at the local nursery. I was two and a half at the time. My parents were relieved when they received a phone call a few weeks later telling them that I had been accepted at the children's nursery centre.

With the new arrival, my parents had to reshape the daily routines that they had worked out together over the previous two years or so. Nursery became a big part of that change. Their days no longer revolved almost entirely around me. I was always a light sleeper, waking several times a night, and was invariably up very early in the mornings. Come breakfast time, my father fed, washed and dressed me while my mother took care of my baby brother. The ride in the buggy to the nursery was an intricate mile long, past the Quaker cemetery where the nineteenth-century prison reformer Elizabeth Fry is buried, and a group of large flats, before coming to an archway leading onto a footpath and a series of street corners.

The nursery was my first experience of the outside world and my own recollections of that time are few but strong, like narrow shards of light piercing through the fog of time. There was the sandpit in which I spent long periods of the day picking and pulling at the sand, fascinated by the individual grains. Then came an obsession with hourglasses (the nursery had several of different sizes) and I remember watching the trickling flow of sand over and over again, oblivious to the children playing around me.

My parents tell me I was a loner, not mixing with the other children, and described by the supervisors as being absorbed in my own world. The contrast between my earliest years and that time must have been vivid for my parents, evolving as I did from a screaming, crying, head banging baby to a quiet, self-absorbed, aloof toddler. With hindsight, they realise now that the change was not necessarily the sign of improvement they took it to be at the time. I became almost too good – too quiet and too undemanding.

Autism as a complex developmental disorder was little known among the general public at this time and my behaviour was not what many assumed then to be typically autistic – I didn't rock my body continuously, I could talk and showed at least some ability to interact with the environment around me. It would be another decade before high-functioning autism, including Asperger's, would start to become recognised within the medical community and gradually better known among the public at large.

There was something else, too. My parents did not want to label me, to feel that they were holding me back in any way. More than anything else, they wanted me to be happy, healthy and able to lead a 'normal' life. When friends, family and neighbours invariably asked about me, my parents told them that I was very 'shy' and 'sensitive'. I think my parents must also have been afraid of the possible stigma attached to having a child with developmental problems.

Another of my memories from my first months at nursery is of the different textures of the floor – some parts were covered in mats, others in carpet. I remember walking slowly, my head firmly down, watching my feet as I trod around the different parts of the floor, experiencing the different sensations under my soles. Because my head was always down when I walked I sometimes bumped into the other children or the assistants at the nursery, but because I moved so slowly the collision was always slight and I would turn a little and carry on regardless.

When the weather was warm and dry outside, the supervisors would let us play in a small garden that was attached to the nursery building. There was a slide and some swings as well as a sprinkling of toys on the grass:

brightly-coloured balls and percussion instruments. There would always be plastic-coated mats placed at the bottom of the slide and under the swings, in case any of the children fell. I loved to walk barefoot on those mats. In hot weather my feet became sweaty and stuck to the mats and I would lift my foot up and put it down again to recreate over and over the sticking sensation on the soles of my feet.

What must the other children have made of me? I don't know, because I have no memory of them at all. To me they were the background to my visual and tactile experiences. I had no sense at all of play as a mutual activity. It seems the workers at the nursery accommodated my unusual behaviour, because they never tried to make me play with the other children. Perhaps they hoped that I would begin to acclimatise to the children around me and interact with them, but I never did.

My father would always drop me off at the nursery and sometimes pick me up too. He would come straight from the factory, often still wearing his work clothes. He wasn't self-conscious at all. He was necessarily a man of many talents. After arriving home, he would change and then make a start on supper. He did most of the cooking; I think it helped him to unwind. I was a picky eater and mostly ate cereal, bread and milk. It was a fight to make me eat my vegetables.

Bedtime was always a struggle – I often ran around or jumped up and down and it took a long time for me

to settle down to sleep. I would insist on the same toy –
a small red rabbit – to sleep in bed with. Sometimes I
wouldn't sleep at all and cried until my parents relented
and let me sleep in their bed with them. When I did fall
asleep, nightmares were common. One example re-
mains with me to this day. I woke up after dreaming of
a huge dragon standing over me. I was tiny in comparison. The same dream recurred night after night. I
became petrified of falling asleep and being eaten by
the dragon. Then one night he was gone as suddenly as
he had appeared. Though I continued to have nightmares, they became gradually less frequent and less
frightening. In a way I had vanquished the dragon.

One morning on the usual route to nursery, my
father decided to take a different turning. To his
surprise I began howling in my buggy. I wasn't yet
three, but I had learnt every detail of the journey from
home to the nursery centre. An old lady walking past
stopped and stared and then remarked: 'He certainly
has a good pair of lungs.' Embarrassed, my father
turned back and went the usual way. In an instant
my crying ceased.

Another memory from my time at the nursery centre
is of watching one of the assistants blow bubbles. Many
of the children stretched their hands out to catch them
as they floated over their heads. I didn't put my hands
out to touch them, but stared at the shape and motion
and the way the light reflected off their shiny, wet
surface. I particularly liked it when the assistant blew

hard and produced a long string of smaller bubbles, one after another in quick succession.

I didn't play with many toys at the centre or back at home. When I did hold a toy, like my rabbit, I would grasp it rigidly at the edges and move it from side to side. There was no attempt at hugging or cuddling or making the rabbit hop. One of my favourite pursuits was taking a coin and spinning it on the floor and watching it as it spun round and round. I would do this over and over, never seeming to get bored.

My parents remember me striking my mother's shoes repetitively against the floor, because I liked the sound they made. I even took to putting them on my feet and walking gingerly around the room with them on. My parents called them my 'clip clop' shoes.

On one of my father's walks down the street with me in the buggy, I called out as we passed a shop window. He was reluctant to take me inside. Normally when my parents were out they never took me inside a shop, because on the few occasions they had done so in the past I had burst into tears and had a tantrum. Each time they had had to make their apologies, 'He's very sensitive,' they would explain, and leave in a hurry. This time my cry seemed different, determined. As my father took me inside he noticed the large display of *Mr Men* books. There was the bright yellow shape of Mr Happy and the purple triangle of Mr Rush. He took one and gave it to me. I wouldn't let go of it so he bought it. The next day we walked past the same shop and I called out again. My father went inside and bought another *Mr Men* book. This soon became a matter of routine, until he had bought me every character in the series.

My *Mr Men* books and I soon became inseparable. I wouldn't leave the house without one. I spent hours in the evenings lying on the floor with the books in my hands, looking at the colours and shapes in the illustrations. My parents were happy to leave me to my obsession with the *Mr Men* characters. For the first time I seemed happy and peaceful. It also proved a useful way of encouraging better behaviour. If I could go a whole day without having a tantrum they would promise to buy me a new *Mr Men* book.

We moved to our first house when I was four. It was at the corner of Blithbury Road. The house was an odd shape with the staircase accessible only from a separate narrow hall adjacent to the living room. The bathroom was downstairs, a short walk from the front door. Sometimes when a family member or friend was visiting they would be surprised by drifting bathtime steam clouds as they entered the house.

My parents' recollections of Blithbury Road are not positive. The kitchen regularly suffered from damp and the house was always cold in winter. Even so, we had good neighbours, including an elderly couple who took a particular shine to my brother and me and gave us sweets and lemonade when we were in the garden.

At the front of the house, my father busied himself at weekends with a vegetable garden, which quickly became filled with potatoes, carrots, peas, onions, kohlrabi, tomatoes, strawberries and rhubarb. On Sunday afternoons we always ate rhubarb and custard for dessert.

I shared my room with my brother. It was small, so to conserve space we had a bunk bed. Though he was two years younger than me, my brother had the top bed. My parents were worried I might get restless in the night and fall out otherwise.

I had no strong feelings towards my brother and we lived parallel lives. He often played in the garden while I stayed in my room and we hardly ever played together. When we did, it was not mutual play – I never felt any sense of wanting to share my toys or experiences with him. Looking back, those feelings seem somewhat alien to me now. I understand the idea of mutuality, of having shared experiences. Though I sometimes still find it difficult to open up and give of myself the feelings necessary to do so are definitely inside me. Perhaps they always were, but it took time for me to find and understand them.

I became an increasingly quiet child and spent most of my time in my room, sitting on my own in a particular spot on the floor, absorbed in the silence. Sometimes I'd press my fingers into my ears to get closer to the silence, which was never static in my mind, but a silky, trickling motion around my head like condensation.

When I closed my eyes I pictured it as soft and silvery. I didn't have to think about it; it would just happen. If there was a sudden noise, such as a knock on the door, it was painful to me, like a shattering of that experience.

The living room downstairs was always filled with books. My parents were both dedicated readers and I can still remember sitting on the floor and watching them with their books, newspapers and magazines in hand. Sometimes, when I was good, I was allowed to sit on their laps while they read. I liked the sound of the pages as they were flicked over. Books became very special to me, because whenever my parents were reading, the room would fill with silence. It made me feel calm and content inside.

I started hoarding my parents' books, carrying them one at a time in my arms up to my room. The stairs were difficult for me and I would negotiate them one step at a time. If the book I was carrying was heavy or large it could take me a full minute to climb a dozen steps. Some of the books were pretty old and smelled of must.

Inside my room I sorted the books into piles on the floor until they surrounded me on all sides. It was hard for my parents to come into the room for fear of knocking one of the piles on top of me. If they tried to remove any of the books I would burst into tears and have a tantrum. The pages of my books all had numbers on them and I felt happy encircled by them, as though wrapped in a numerical comfort blanket. Long before I could read the sentences on the pages, I could count the numbers. And when I counted, the numbers would appear as motions or coloured shapes in my mind.

On one expedition up the stairs with my arms clasping a particularly heavy book I slipped and fell. The falling motion seemed to fill my mind with rapid flashes of bright and sketchy colour, like scattered sunlight. I just sat at the bottom of the stairs, dazzled and sore. I didn't think to call for help but waited for my father to come and see what the noise was. I rarely if ever spoke unless spoken to. After that, my parents started hiding their larger and heavier books from me, afraid that I would fall again and hurt myself badly.

There was a park close enough to the house to visit on foot so we went there most weekends. My parents tore up slices of bread for me to throw to the ducks. They usually took us early in the mornings when there were few people about. They knew that I was frightened by the presence of lots of people. While my brother ran around, I sat on my own on the ground, pulling up the blades of grass and picking the petals off the daisies.

My favourite experience at the park was going on the swings. My father would pick me up and sit me down on the swing and push me gently. When he got tired and stopped pushing me I would shout 'more . . . more' until he started pushing again. There was also a roundabout, and I sat in the middle of it as my parents stood either side and slowly moved it round. As the roundabout spun I closed my eyes and smiled. It made me feel good.

The road near the park was sometimes noisy as we walked back home. If a passing car made a sudden, loud noise – like a blaring horn – I would stop and throw my hands up and press them hard against my ears. Often the noise was more sudden than it was loud. It was because it was unexpected that it seemed to affect me so much. It is for this reason that I hated balloons and would cower if I saw someone holding one. I was frightened that it would burst and make a loud and violent noise.

After our move to Blithbury Road, until the age of five I continued my nursery at a local school called Dorothy Barley, named after a sixteenth-century abbess who lived in the area during the reign of Henry VIII. We were often given paper and coloured pencils by the nursery assistants and encouraged to draw and colour in. I always enjoyed this, though I found it difficult to hold the pencil between my fingers and would grip it with my palm. I liked drawing circles of lots of different sizes. The circle was my favourite shape and I drew it over and over again.

The nursery had a box in the corner full of lots of things to play with. My favourites were the coloured beads I found; I would hold them in my hands and shake them to watch them vibrate around my palms. If we were given cardboard rolls to play with (to make binoculars or a telescope, for example) I would drop the beads through the roll, fascinated that the beads dropped through one end and fell out of the other. If I found a tub or jar I would drop the beads inside and then empty it and begin again.

On one wall was a shelf with a selection of books. My favourite was *The Very Hungry Caterpillar*. I loved the holes in the pages and the bright, round illustrations. There was a reading corner nearby where the children sat on a large mat around the assistant and listened to a book being read to them. On one such occasion, I was sitting near the back with my legs crossed and my head down, absorbed in my own world. I didn't hear a word of what was being said. Instead, without realising it, I began to hum. As I looked up, the assistant had stopped reading and everyone was staring at me. I stopped humming and put my head back down and the reading resumed.

I don't remember feeling lonely at the nursery, probably because I was so absorbed in my books and beads and circles. Slowly I think the feeling was creeping over me that I was different from the other children, but for some reason it didn't bother me. I didn't yet feel any desire for friends; I was happy enough playing by myself.

When the time came to play social games, such as musical chairs, I refused to join in. I was frightened by the thought of the other children touching me as they shoved one another for one of the remaining seats. No amount of gentle persuasion by the supervisors would work. Instead I was allowed to stand by one of the walls and watch the other children play. So long as I was left to myself I was happy.

The moment I came home from the nursery I would always go upstairs to my room. Whenever I was feeling tired or upset I would crawl into the darkness under the bed and lie there. My parents learnt to tap quietly at the door before coming in to see how I was. My mother always made me tell her about my day at the nursery. She wanted to encourage me to speak, because I was so quiet so much of the time.

My room was my sanctuary, my personal space where I felt most comfortable and happy. I spent so much of my day there that my parents took to coming up and sitting with me in order to spend time with me. They never seemed impatient with me.

As I sit here now and write about those early years, I'm amazed to think how much my parents did for me even as they must have got so little back at the time. Hearing their recollections of my earliest years has been a magical experience for me; to see for myself in hindsight the extent of their role in making me the person I am today. In spite of all my many problems, all the tears and tantrums and other difficulties, they loved me unconditionally and devoted themselves to helping me – little by little, day by day. They are my heroes.

3

Struck by Lightning: Epilepsy

I was sitting on the living room floor when it happened. I was four years old and sat with my brother Lee while my father was making dinner in the kitchen. It was not exceptional at that age for me to feel moments of complete disconnection, periods of total self-absorption – studying closely the lines on the palms of my hands or watching my shifting shadow as I leaned backwards and forwards in slow and rhythmic movements. But this was something else, an experience unlike any other, as though the room around me was pulling away from me on all sides and the light inside it leaking out and the flow of time itself coagulated and stretched out into a single lingering moment. I did not and could not have known it then, but I was having a massive epileptic seizure.

Epilepsy is one of the most common conditions affecting the brain – around 300,000 people in the UK have some form of it. Seizures are the result of brief electrical disturbances in the brain. Little is presently known about why they happen or how they start and stop. No single apparent cause has been found, but doctors think that epilepsy may be due to a problem with the links between nerve cells or the balance of chemicals in the brain.

In the days before the seizure my father had noticed my eyes flicker and arms tense as I lay on the settee in the living room watching television. He was concerned and called the doctor to come and examine me. The weather was hot and humid and the doctor suggested that I might only have had a 'turn'. He recommended that my father remain vigilant and immediately report any further such episodes.

I was extremely fortunate that my brother was with me at the time of the second seizure. I had gone into convulsions and lost consciousness. My father, hearing my brother crying, rushed in to find the cause of the commotion. Acting on instinct, he carefully scooped me up into his arms and ran out of the house to a row of taxicabs parked close by. Climbing inside the first, he begged the driver to take him to the nearest hospital – St George's – as quickly as possible. As the taxi raced through the streets, there was nothing my father could do but hold me close to him and pray.

Sweating profusely, my father ran from the taxi straight to the children's ward. I had not come round and the seizure activity continued, a potentially life-threatening condition known as 'status epilepticus'. A nurse at reception collected me from my father's arms and called for doctors who first gave me a valium injection to help stabilise my condition. I was not breathing and had started to turn blue, so the doctors performed cardiopulmonary resuscitation (CPR) to revive me. It was about an hour after the seizure had begun that my condition started finally to return to normal. Exhausted by the ordeal, my father burst into tears of relief at the news. He had by his prompt action helped save my life.

I was diagnosed with temporal lobe epilepsy. The temporal lobes are located on the side of the head above the ears. They are deeply involved with sensory input, memory, hearing and perception, and seizures occurring in this area of the brain can impair memory function and affect personality.

The prevalence of epilepsy among those on the autistic spectrum is much higher than in the normal population. About a third of children with an autistic spectrum disorder develop temporal lobe epilepsy by adolescence. For this reason it is thought that the two conditions may have a common source in the brain's structure or in the genetics that underlie it.

As part of the diagnosis, I was given a test called an electroencephalogram (EEG). During an EEG, electrodes are placed around the scalp to measure the brain's electrical activity and to check for any abnormalities in the brain waves. I recall the technician standing over me and sticking the electrodes – small and circular metal caps – on to different parts of my head with paste to keep them in place. I winced and grimaced as each one was applied because I didn't like the sensation of someone touching my head.

I also underwent a magnetic resonance imaging (MRI) brain scan. MRI uses a powerful large magnet, microwave radiation and computers to generate detailed images of the inside of the body. I was sedated ahead of the scan, probably because the technician was concerned that I would not be able to cope with the noise of the machine and the possible feeling of claustrophobia while inside the scanner. I remember being laid down on a soft, bright white couch which was then pushed into a narrow tunnel for the scan, which lasted around thirty minutes. I must have fallen asleep inside because I remember being woken by my father after the couch was pulled out from the tunnel. This is in spite of the fact that the scanner would have been very noisy while the pictures were being taken.

I stayed in hospital for several days while the different tests were being carried out. My parents took it in turns to stay with me day and night. They were frightened that I might wake up and panic if I did not see a familiar face. The ward where I stayed had a shiny floor with lots of tiny scratches on it and the texture of the sheets on my bed felt different to those at home – pricklier and less soft. My parents gave me orange juice to drink and colouring-in books and crayons to occupy myself with, but a lot of the time I just spent sleeping because I felt so tired.

The doctors told my parents that my prognosis was good – about half of all children diagnosed with temporal lobe epilepsy outgrow the condition. I was prescribed anti-seizure medication and allowed home.

Being diagnosed with epilepsy affected both my parents very deeply, my father in particular. His father – my grandfather – had suffered from epileptic seizures over many years in adulthood and died prematurely several years before I was born.

His name was William John Edward and he was born in East London in the early 1900s. He had worked as a shoe repairer and fought during the Second World War, evacuated from Dunkirk before being stationed at a military base in northern Scotland, manning an anti-aircraft gun. He was married and had four children; my father was the youngest. The seizures began after the war and were particularly violent – my grandmother quickly became familiar with the sound of crashing plates and cups being knocked from the kitchen table on to the floor.

At that time the resources available for helping those living with epilepsy were limited. Doctors suggested that my grandfather's illness had been brought on by shell shock suffered during the war. They advised my grandmother to divorce her husband and to move on. After all, she had a young family and her whole life ahead of her. It must have been the most difficult decision she ever had to make, but she took the doctors' advice and subsequently remarried. My grandfather was moved to a long-stay institution for ex-soldiers with mental problems.

The break-up of my grandparents' relationship had disastrous consequences for the family. My grandmother started a new family but her second husband struggled to find work and gambled what little he earned so that, without a stable income, they soon found themselves with growing rent arrears. One day the family returned home to find their furniture piled up on the lawn and the doors padlocked. They had been evicted by the council for non-payment of rent – they were homeless.

A friend of the family initially took the children in, including my father who had the role of eldest brother to his stepsiblings, before they were moved with my grandmother to a hostel for the homeless. My father was given a Lego set as a going-away present by the family friend who had helped to look after him. The hostel was made up of small huts with shared toilets, bathroom and kitchen for the residents. The corridors connecting the rooms were narrow and the floor was covered in red concrete. My father could hear the members of staff walking along the corridor from the noise of their footsteps. He nicknamed one 'Jackboots'.

The family's accommodation consisted of two cramped, unfurnished rooms. No television or radios were allowed. In one room – the children's – there was space for three small beds. My grandmother's room had a bed, table and chair. No men were allowed to stay, so her husband was forced to rent rooms above a shop. They would be separated for the duration of the family's stay at the hostel.

Life at the hostel was grim – apart from the bare accommodation, there was no privacy; doors were to remain unlocked at all times, and the staff were strict and ran the building in a military fashion. The family hated their time there, which lasted for a year and a half. Their stay was only brightened a little by the friendship my grandmother was able to strike up with the hostel manager, a Mrs Jones. Eventually, the family was moved to a new house.

My father met his father for the first time when he was eleven. By then my grandfather's seizures were less frequent and he was allowed out on day release to work at his shoe repair shop. In the evenings he returned to the institution. My father had been very young when my grandfather's illness began, so he had no memories of him and did not even know what he looked like. They met at the home of the family friend who had helped care for him and his stepsiblings several years earlier. My father remembers shaking hands with a grey-haired man with ill-fitting clothes who was then introduced to him as his father. Over time, they grew close.

As my grandfather got older his health quickly deteriorated. My father would visit him at the hospital as often as he could. He was twenty-one when my grandfather died, of organ failure following a stroke and seizure. From all accounts he was a kind and gentle man. I wish I could have had the opportunity to meet him.

I am extremely fortunate to live in an age of many important medical advances, so that my own experience of epilepsy was nothing like that of my grandfather's. Following the seizures and my diagnosis, I think what must have frightened my parents most of all was the possibility that I would not be able to lead the 'normal' life they really wanted for me. Like many parents, they equated normality with being happy and productive.

The seizures did not recur – as is the case in around 80% of those living with epilepsy, my medication was effective which meant I lived seizure-free. I think this was the biggest factor in my mother's ability to cope with my illness. She was very sensitive to the fact that somehow I had always been different, vulnerable, in need of extra care and support and love. Sometimes she got upset at the thought that I could have another seizure at any time. Then she would go into another room and cry softly. I remember my father telling me not to go into the room when my mother was upset.

I found it very hard to pick up on my mother's feelings. It didn't help that I remained in my own world, engrossed in the smallest things but unable to understand the various emotions or tensions at home. My parents sometimes fought, as I think most parents do, over their children and the best way to deal with different situations. When they argued, their voices turned a dark blue colour in my mind and I would crouch on the floor and press my forehead into the carpet with my hands over my ears until the noise abated.

It was my father who helped me to take my tablets every day, with a glass of milk or water around meal-times. The medication – carbamazepine – meant I had to go with him to the hospital every month for blood tests, because of the effect the tablets can sometimes have on liver function. My father is a stickler for punctuality and we were always at the hospital waiting area at least an hour before the appointment was due. He would buy me a plastic cup of orange juice and some cookies while we waited. The chairs that we sat on were plastic and uncomfortable but I remember not wanting to stand up on my own, so I waited for my father to stand before I did. There were lots of chairs and I passed the time by counting them over and over.

When the nurse called my name, my father walked with me to a small curtained-off area where I sat down and the nurse rolled up one of my sleeves and dabbed the centre of my arm. I had many blood tests so that with time I knew what to expect. The nurse encouraged patients to look away while the needle was being inserted but I kept my head still, my gaze fixed, watching the transparent tube above the needle fill with dark red blood. Once she was finished, the nurse dabbed the arm clean and stuck cotton wool in place with a plaster that had a smiley face on it.

One of the commonest side effects of the medication is hypersensitivity to sunlight and I spent the summer months indoors while my brother played outside in the garden and the park. I didn't mind because, even today, sunlight often makes me feel itchy and uncomfortable and I rarely venture outside for long periods in sunny weather. My parents wanted to supervise me even more closely following the seizures so I spent a lot of time in the living room, where my mother could keep a close eye on me, watching television or playing with coins or beads I was given to count with.

Feelings of dizziness or grogginess were also common side effects I experienced. Whenever I started to feel dizzy I would immediately sit down, cross my legs and wait for the sensation to pass. This sometimes caused embarrassment for my parents if they were walking with me in the street and I suddenly stopped and sat down in the middle of the pavement. Fortunately the dizzy spells did not last long, just a matter of seconds. The loss of control, as well as the unpredictability of the spells, frightened me and I was often tetchy and tearful following one.

There exists a complex relationship between sleep and epilepsy, with a higher incidence of sleep disorders found among those with the condition. Some scientists believe that sleep-related events such as sleep terrors and sleepwalking may actually represent nocturnal seizure activity in the brain. I occasionally sleepwalked – in some periods frequently, in others less – from around the age of six through to the start of my adolescence. Sleepwalking (somnambulism) occurs during the first three hours of sleep, when the sleeper's brain waves have increased in size and the sleep is dreamless and deep. Typically, the sleepwalker does not respond if talked to and does not remember the episode upon waking. In my case, I would climb out of bed and walk repetitively in the same path around my room. Sometimes I would bang into the walls or door in my room, waking my parents who would gently guide me back to bed. Though it's not in fact harmful to wake someone who is sleepwalking, it can be confusing and upsetting for the sleepwalker.

My parents took several precautions to ensure my safety during the night. They cleared the floor of my room of any toys each evening before bed and left a light on in the hallway when it came to bedtime. They also fitted a gate at the top of the stairs after one occasion when I apparently sleepwalked down the stairs and to the back of the house and was found pulling at the kitchen door leading out to the garden.

Perhaps not surprisingly, during the day it frequently felt like all my energy had been emptied away and all I wanted to do was sleep. It was normal for me to put my head down on my school desk in class and fall asleep. The teachers, fully informed by my parents, were always sympathetic and tolerant. It was often disorientating to wake up after a period of ten or twenty or thirty minutes and find the class empty and the children running outside in the playground, but my teacher was always there to reassure me.

The cumulative impact of the various side effects of my medication on my first year at school was considerable. I found it hard to concentrate in class, or to work at a consistent pace. I was the last child in the class to master my ABC. My teacher, Mrs Lemon, gave me extra encouragement with coloured stickers if I made fewer and fewer mistakes as I wrote the alphabet down. I never felt self-conscious or embarrassed at lagging behind the other children; they just weren't a part of my world.

Twice a year I visited the Westminster Children's Hospital in London with my father for a brain scan to monitor my condition. We would go by taxi, arrive early as usual, and then wait for the consultant to call us. I must have spent many, many hours over those years sitting in hospital waiting areas.

After three years the decision was made to gradually

phase out my anti-seizure medication. My mother panicked at the thought that the epilepsy might return, though fortunately I remained and remain today seizure-free. The previous side effects of the medication disappeared and my performance at school improved thereafter.

It's not clear what lasting effect – if any – the epilepsy has had on my brain and how it works. My childhood seizures originated in the left temporal lobe and some researchers suggest that one explanation for savant abilities is left brain injury leading to right brain compensation. This is because the skills most commonly seen in savants, including numbers and calculation, are associated with the right hemisphere.

However, it is not easy to determine whether the epilepsy is a cause or a symptom of the left brain injury and it is possible that my seizures in childhood came about as a consequence of pre-existing damage in the brain, probably there from birth.

For this reason, scientists have been interested in studying my perception abilities to see in what way they differ from those of other people. A study was carried out at the Autism Research Centre in Cambridge in the autumn of 2004. The centre's director is Simon Baron-Cohen, a professor of developmental psychopathology and a leading researcher into autistic spectrum disorders.

The study tested the 'weak central coherence' theory,

which says that individuals on the autistic spectrum are more likely to process details at the expense of global information ('the bigger picture'), whereas most people integrate information into context and gist – often missing out on smaller details. For example, studies have shown that autistic children are better at recognising familiar faces in photographs when given just part of the face than are non-autistic controls.

In the Navon task, participants are asked to identify a selected target occurring at either a local or global level. In my test at the centre, the scientists asked me to press a button by my left hand if I saw a letter 'A' and to press a button by my right hand if I didn't. Images were flashed up onto a screen in front of me and responses were automatic. On several occasions I pressed 'no', only for my brain to catch up seconds later with the perception that the overall configuration of the letters created an 'A' shape. Scientists call this phenomenon 'interference' and it is commonly employed in optical illusions. For most people, the interference is caused by the global shape – for example, when presented with a letter 'H' composed of lots of small 'A's, most people will not immediately see the 'A's because of the interference effect of seeing the 'H' shape. In my case, like those of most people on the autistic spectrum, the interference is reversed and I struggle to see the overall letter shape because my brain focuses automatically on the individual details.

```
    H              A           A
  H  H             A           A
 H    H            A           A
HHHH           A A A A
 H      H          A           A
H          H       A           A
```

In the above illustrations the image on the left shows the letter 'A' composed of smaller 'H's. The right image shows the letter 'H' composed of smaller 'A's.

In Australia, Professor Allan Snyder – director of the Centre for the Mind at the University of Sydney – has attracted considerable interest for his claims that he can reproduce savant-like abilities in subjects using a technique called transcranial magnetic stimulation (TMS).

TMS has been used as a medical tool in brain surgery, stimulating or suppressing particular areas of the brain to allow doctors to monitor the effects of surgery in real time. It is non-invasive and seemingly free of serious side effects.

Professor Snyder believes that autistic thought is not wholly different to ordinary thought, but an extreme form of it. By temporarily inhibiting some brain activity – the ability to think contextually and conceptually, for example – TMS, Professor Snyder argues, can be used to induce heightened access to parts of the brain responsible for collecting raw, unfiltered information.

By doing this, he hopes to enhance the brain by shutting off certain parts of it, changing the way the subject perceives different things.

The professor uses a cap attached by electrodes to a TMS machine. The machine sends varying pulses of magnetic energy to the temporal lobes. Some of the subjects who have undergone the procedure claim temporarily enhanced drawing and proofreading skills; drawings of animals became more life-like and detailed, and reading became more precise.

Most people read by recognising familiar groupings of words. For this reason, many miss small errors of spelling or word repetition. Take the following example:

> A bird in the hand
> is worth two in the
> the bush

Read quickly, most people don't spot the second, superfluous 'the' in the sentence above.

A side benefit of processing information in parts instead of holistically is that having a good eye for detail, I proofread very well. On Sunday mornings, reading pages of the day's newspaper at the table, I would annoy my parents no end by pointing out every grammatical and spelling error I found. 'Why can't you just read the paper like everyone else?' my exasperated mother would ask, having listened to me point out the twelfth error in the paper.

Professor Snyder argues that savant abilities may be in everyone, only most are unable to unlock them. He believes my epileptic seizures may have played a role, similar to that of the magnetic energy pulses of his TMS machine, in affecting certain areas of my brain, paving the way for my abilities with numbers and different perceptual processing.

There are examples of those who have acquired savant skills following illness or injury to the brain. One is Orlando Serrell who was hit on the head by a baseball at the age of ten. Several months later he started recalling huge amounts of information, including licence-plate numbers, song lyrics and weather reports.

Similar transformations have been reported in cases of patients suffering from frontotemporal dementia (FTD), a degenerative brain disease affecting the frontal and temporal lobes. As the disease progresses, personality, behaviour and memory are affected. FTD mostly occurs in adults in their forties, fifties and sixties.

Bruce Miller, a neurologist at the University of California in San Francisco, says some of his patients with FTD spontaneously develop interest and skill in art and music. Studies using brain imaging show that for those patients who develop skills, blood flow or metabolic activity is much reduced to the left temporal lobe. Meanwhile, the right hemisphere of the brain, where visual and spatial processing is located, is much better preserved.

It seems that my childhood seizures may well have played an important role in making me the person I am today. Many others have felt similarly about their experience of epilepsy, among them Fyodor Dostoevsky. The nineteenth-century Russian writer – author of such literary classics as *Crime and Punishment* and *The Brothers Karamazov* – had a rare form of temporal lobe epilepsy called 'Ecstatic Epilepsy'. Dostoevsky's seizures mostly occured at night and were generalised, affecting his entire body. His experience of epilepsy led him to create characters with epilepsy in four of his novels: Kirilov in *The Possessed*, Smerdyakov in *The Brothers Karamazov*, Nellie in *The Insulted and Injured* and Prince Myshkin in *The Idiot*.

Dostoevsky described his experience of epilepsy in this way:

> For several instants I experience a happiness that is impossible in an ordinary state, and of which other people have no conception. I feel full harmony in myself and in the whole world, and the feeling is so strong and sweet that for a few seconds of such bliss one could give up ten years of life, perhaps all of life.
>
> I felt that heaven descended to earth and swallowed me. I really attained god and was imbued with him. All of you healthy people don't even suspect what happiness is, that happiness that we epileptics experience for a second before an attack.

The writer and mathematician Lewis Carroll is also thought to have had temporal lobe seizures, which may have inspired the writing of his most famous work, *Alice's Adventures in Wonderland*. The following passage describes an experience of falling involuntarily, which is very similar to that of an epileptic seizure:

> Alice had not a moment to think about stopping herself before she found herself falling down a very deep well . . . 'Well!' thought Alice to herself, 'after such a fall as this, I shall think nothing of tumbling down stairs!' . . . down, down, down. Would the fall never come to an end?

Some researchers even believe there may be a link between epilepsy and creativity. Writer Eve LaPlante makes this case in her book *Seized: Temporal Lobe Epilepsy as a Medical, Historical and Artistic Phenomenon*. In it, she cites the famous case of the painter Vincent Van Gogh, who suffered from severe seizures that left him depressed, confused and agitated. In spite of his illness, Van Gogh produced hundreds of watercolours, oil paintings and drawings.

For several months around the age of eight I wrote compulsively across long reams of computer paper, often writing for hours at a time, covering sheet after sheet of paper with tightly knit words. My parents had to buy huge rolls of paper for me because I kept running out. My handwriting was tiny – one teacher complained that she had had to change the prescription of her glasses to read my work – as a result of my fear of running out of paper on which to write down the words.

The stories I wrote, from what I can remember of them, were descriptively dense – a whole page might be taken up in describing the various details of a single place or location, its colours, shapes and textures. There was no dialogue, no emotions. Instead I wrote of long, weaving tunnels far underneath vast, shimmering oceans, of cragged rock caves and towers climbing high into the sky.

I didn't have to think about what I was writing; the words just seemed to flow out of my head. Even without any conscious planning, the stories were always comprehensible. When I showed one to my teacher, she liked it enough to read parts of it out loud to the rest of the class. My compulsion to write soon disappeared as suddenly as it had first visited me. However, it left me with a permanent fascination for words and language – something which has since been greatly beneficial to me.

More and more people today living with epilepsy are able to lead seizure-free lives, thanks to the ongoing advances in medicine and technology. The stigma that was once attached to those diagnosed with conditions such as epilepsy (and autism) is rapidly disappearing. In spite of this, disorders affecting the brain are still misunderstood by many people. I would tell parents with children who have been diagnosed with epilepsy to educate themselves as much as possible about the condition. Most important of all, give your children the self-belief to hold on to their dreams, because they are the things that shape each person's future.

4

Schooldays

School began for me in September 1984, just as my
brother Lee was starting nursery. My father walked
me to class in the mornings – sometimes impatiently
because I walked so slowly and kept stopping to pick
up stones to hold between my fingers. My teacher,
Mrs Lemon, was a tall, thin lady with short dark
hair. I liked her name because whenever I heard it I
would immediately picture the shape and colour of
the fruit. 'Lemon' was one of the first words I ever
learnt to write.

Next to the school entrance gates there was a cloak-
room for the children to put their coats in before going

into class. I didn't very much like using it because there
was only one small window high up in the wall and the
room was always gloomy. I was so terrified of losing my
coat among all the others, or of picking up a similar
looking one and taking it home with me, that I took to
counting the pegs to work out which one was mine. If
ever I came in and found my peg already occupied I
would get upset and panic. I remember once walking
straight into class with my coat still on because my peg
had another child's coat on it, even though there were
lots of other free pegs to hang my coat on.

The classroom was rectangular and was entered
from the right side. Inside there were rows upon rows
of drawers for the children to put their pencils and
paper into, each labelled with the child's full name. We
were each given a plastic folder that also had a name
label, stuck onto the top left hand corner. The folder
had a coloured zip at the top to open and close it and
we were told to keep our reading books and work inside
it. I used mine with fastidious care – always remembering to return my books to it once I had finished with
them.

My desk was near the back of the classroom next to
the window, which was plastered in coloured paper
and pupils' drawings, from where I could look over the
other children in the class and not have to make eye
contact with any of them. I don't recall the names or
faces of any of the children from my first years at
school – I always felt them to be something to cope and

contend with, to navigate around, rather than as individuals to get to know and to play with.

I often held my hands together at chest height when I
was standing or walking in class. Sometimes I'd fold
my fingers over, then uncurl one or another and just
stand there with one or more of my fingers pointing
up towards the class ceiling. One time I pointed my
middle finger and was surprised when a boy came up
to me and said I was swearing. 'How can a finger
swear?' I asked, but instead of replying the boy called
loudly for the teacher who promptly told me off for
rude behaviour.

Assemblies in the morning were something I grew
to really enjoy. For one thing they were predictable,
occurring at the same time each morning. The teacher
would ask us to stand in alphabetical order outside the
classroom, then walk in line to the assembly hall.
Inside, children from the other classes sat quietly in
straight lines as we walked past, before being told to sit
ourselves down behind the others. The strong sense of
order and routine calmed me and I often sat on the hall
floor with my eyes closed, gently rocking while
humming to myself – something I frequently did when
I was feeling relaxed and content.

The best part of each assembly came with the singing
of hymns: 'He's Got the Whole World in His Hands'
and 'Oats, Peas, Beans and Barley Grow' were among
my favourites. I closed my eyes and listened intently to
the other children singing together, the notes melting

together into a reassuringly steady, flowing rhythm. The music always made me feel at peace and happy inside. Assembly time was the highlight of my school day.

With my first Christmas at school came the traditional Nativity play. I was given the role of one of the shepherds. I was petrified at the thought of having to stand up in front of the whole school – all the children and teachers and parents – and became very distressed, refusing to try on the shepherd's costume or to talk things over with the teacher. In the end, my mother intervened by bribing me with sweets in return for my participation. I looked down at the floor the whole time I was on stage, but it didn't stop my parents from telling me afterwards how proud of me they were. After the play I didn't want to get out of the costume, so my parents persuaded my teacher to lend it to them over the Christmas break. That night, and every one after until New Year, I slept in my shepherd's robes and hat.

Learning in class did not come easily to me – I found it difficult to concentrate when the other children were talking among themselves or when there were people walking or running in the corridors outside. I find it very hard to filter out external noise and regularly put my fingers in my ears to help me concentrate. My brother Steven has the same problem and uses earplugs whenever he wants to read or think.

Whenever I wrote, I pored over every letter and word

and full stop. If I noticed a smudge or error I would rub everything out and start over. This streak of perfectionism meant that I sometimes worked at a snail's pace, finishing a lesson in a state of near exhaustion, yet with little to show for it. Even so, I never worried that the teacher would consider me lazy or incapable and I never thought to care what any of the other children might think. I didn't then understand the concept of learning from your mistakes.

Writing was always a chore. Certain letters, 'g' and 'k' in particular, were tiresome to write down because I just couldn't remember how to write them. I practised writing out whole lines of 'g's and 'k's on sheet after sheet of paper to help me, but their loops and 'arms' seemed unintuitive to me and it was a long time before I was able to write them with confidence. I lagged behind in handwriting, unable to write words with the letters all connected together. If single letters were difficult enough, combinations such as 'gh' and 'th' were impossible for me to write in a single stroke. Even today I write most of the letters in a word individually one after the other.

One of the items everyone in class was given to take home regularly with them was an old tin filled with strips of paper. On each strip was a different word to be practised, and there were tests each week to see how well the words had been learned. I always scored very well in these tests because I was able to visualise each word in my head, based on the shape its letters formed. The word 'dog', for example, is made up of three circles with an upward line on the first letter and a downward loop on the last. The word actually looks quite a lot like a dog if you imagine the upward line as the dog's ear and the downward loop as the tail. Similarly, the two 'o's in 'look' reminded me of a pair of eyes. Palindromes – words spelt the same backwards as well as forwards – such as 'mum' and 'noon' felt especially beautiful to me and they were among my favourite words.

From about the time I first started school I developed a great love for and fascination with fairy tales – the stories and intricately detailed illustrations filled my head with vivid mental pictures of towns overflowing with porridge and of princesses sleeping on a bed a hundred mattresses high (with a single pea underneath). One of my favourite tales was the famous 'Rumpelstiltskin' by the Brothers Grimm. At bedtime I loved hearing my parents read out the exotic-sounding names guessed by the Queen as the name of the gold-spinning little man: Kasper, Melchior, Belshazzar, Sheepshanks, Cruickshanks, Spindleshanks . . .

Another story that really affected me was 'Stone Soup'. In it, a wandering soldier arrives in a village asking for food and shelter. The villagers, greedy and fearful, provide none, so the soldier declares that he will make them stone soup with nothing required but a cauldron, water and a stone. The villagers huddle round as the soldier begins to cook his dish, licking his lips in anticipation. 'Of course, stone soup with cabbage is hard to beat,' says the soldier to himself in a loud voice. One of the villagers approaches and puts one of his cabbages into the pot. Then the soldier says: 'Once I had stone soup with cabbage and a bit of salt beef and it was fit for a king!' Sure enough, the village butcher brings some salt beef and one by one the other villagers provide potatoes, onions, carrots, mushrooms, and so on until a delicious meal is ready for the entire village. I found the story very puzzling at the time because I had no concept of deception and did not understand that the soldier was pretending to make a soup from a stone in order to trick the villagers into contributing to it. Only many years later did I finally understand what the story was about.

But some fantasy was just too frightening for me. Once a week a television was wheeled into the classroom and an educational programme played. *Look and Read* was a popular BBC children's television series and one of its most watched programmes was *Dark Towers* involving a young girl who, alongside her dog, race to find the hidden treasure of a strange, old house called Dark Towers. The series was played over ten weeks.

In its first episode, the young girl – Tracy – discovers Dark Towers and learns that it is supposed to be haunted. At the end of the episode a family portrait begins to shake and the room goes very cold. Tracy hears a voice telling her that the house is in danger and she will help to save it. I remember watching the programme with the rest of the class in silence, my legs together rocking quietly under the chair. I felt no emotion at all until the end, then all of a sudden it was like a switch was flicked in my head and I suddenly realised I was frightened. Feeling agitated I ran from the class – refusing to return until the television was removed. Thinking back, I can understand why the other children teased me and called me 'cry baby'. I was nearly seven and none of the other children in the class were the slightest bit upset or frightened by the programme. Even so, each week I was taken to the headmaster's office and allowed to sit and wait while the rest of the class watched the next instalment of the series. The headmaster had a small television in his office and I remember watching motor racing on it – the cars were going very fast round and round and round the circuit; this, at least, was a programme I could watch.

Another *Look and Read* series that I remember affected me very much was called *Through the Dragon's Eye*. In it, three children walk through a mural they have painted on the playground wall and into a strange land called Pelamar. The land is dying and the children seek to mend its life force, a glowing, hexagonal structure that has been thrown apart in an explosion. With the help of a friendly dragon called Gorwen, the children search the land for the missing parts.

This time there were no tantrums. For one thing I

was older, ten, but the programme itself was what fascinated me. It was beautifully visual, the children surrounded by various richly coloured landscapes as they made their way across the magical land. Several of the series' characters – keepers of the life force – were painted from head to toe in bright colours of purple, orange and green. Then there was the huge talking mouse and the giant caterpillar. In one scene, snow-flakes fall from the air and are caught in the children's hands, magically transforming into letters which form words (a clue to help the children find one of the missing life force pieces). In another, stars in the night sky light up into shining road signs for the flying dragon Gorwen. Scenes like these fascinated me be-cause the story was told primarily in pictures, which I could relate to best, rather than spoken dialogue.

Watching the television at home became a regular part of my after-school routine. My mother recalls that I always sat very close to the set and became upset if she tried to make me move back a little to protect my eyes. Even in hot weather I always kept my coat on after coming home from school and wore it all the time that I was watching the different programmes, sometimes even longer. I thought of it as an extra protective layer against the outside world, like a knight and his suit of armour.

Meanwhile, the family was growing. My parents were not at all religious, they simply loved children, and always wanted to have a large family. A sister, Claire, was born in the month that I began school, followed two years later by the arrival of my second brother Steven. Shortly afterwards my mother discovered she was pregnant again with her fifth child, my brother Paul, and it became necessary for us to move to a larger house. I had little reaction at first to the growing band of siblings, sitting and playing by myself in the quiet of my bedroom while my brothers and sister shouted and played and ran around downstairs and in the garden. Their presence did ultimately have a very positive influence on me, however: it forced me to gradually develop my social skills. Having people constantly around me helped me to cope better with noise and change. I also began to learn how to interact with other children by silently watching my siblings playing with each other and their friends from my bedroom window.

We moved in the middle of 1987 to Hedingham Road, number forty-three. Interestingly, all three of my childhood addresses were prime numbers: 5, 43, 181. Even better, each of our next-door neighbours had primes on their front doors too: 3 (and 7), 41, 179. Such number pairs are called 'twin primes' – prime numbers that differ by two. Twin primes become rarer the higher you count, so for example finding prime number neighbours with door numbers starting with '9' would require a very long street indeed; the first such pair is 9,011 and 9,013.

The year of our move was also marked by rare severe

weather. January saw some of the coldest weather in southern England for over a hundred years, with temperatures falling to minus nine degrees in some places. The cold brought heavy snowfall and days off school. Outside the children were throwing snowballs and being pulled along on sleds, but I was content to sit at my window and watch the snowflakes falling and fluttering from the sky. Later, when everyone else had gone indoors, I ventured out alone and piled the snow in the front garden into identical pillars several feet high. Looking down from my bedroom they formed a circle – my favourite shape. A neighbour came over to the house and said to my parents: 'Your son has made Stonehenge in the snow.'

1987 was also the year of the great October storm – the worst to affect the south east of England since 1703. Winds reached 100mph in places and eighteen people died as a result of the storm damage. That night I went to bed but found it hard to sleep. My parents had recently bought me a new pair of pyjamas, but the fabric was itchy and I kept turning in bed. I woke to a breaking sound – tiles were being ripped from the roof by the wind and thrown down onto the street below. I climbed onto the windowsill and looked out: everywhere was pitch black. It was warm, too, unusually for the time of year, and my hands were sweaty and stuck to the sill as I pulled myself off. Then I heard a creaking noise coming towards my room. The door opened and in came a trembling, orange light atop a thick, long white candle. I stared at it until a voice, my mother's, asked me if I was all right. I did not say anything because she was holding the candle out in front of her and I wondered whether she was giving it to me, like the bright red candle on a cake she had given me for my last birthday, but I didn't want it because it wasn't my birthday yet.

'Do you want some hot milk?'

I nodded and followed her slowly downstairs to the kitchen. It was dark everywhere, because the power had been cut and none of the light switches worked. I sat up at the table with my mother and drank the frothy milk she had prepared and poured into my favourite mug – it was patterned all over with coloured dots and I used it for every drink. After being led back upstairs to my room I climbed into bed, pulled the covers over my head and fell back to sleep.

In the morning I was woken by my father and told there would be no school that day. Looking out of my bedroom window, I could see broken roof tiles and dustbin lids scattered over the street and people talking in small groups and shaking their heads.

Downstairs, the family was crowded in the kitchen looking out on the garden at the back of the house. The large tree at the bottom of the garden had been ripped out of the ground by the storm's winds, its branches and roots splayed across the grass. It was several weeks before the tree could be sawn up and removed. In the interim I spent many happy hours alone climbing around the tree trunk and hiding among its branches, invariably returning indoors covered in dirt, bugs and scratches.

The house in Hedingham Road was just across the street from my school. I could see the teachers' car park from my bedroom window, which made me feel safe. Every day after school I would run to my bedroom to watch the cars drive away. I counted them one by one as they left, and remembered each number plate. Only once the last cars had gone did I climb down and go downstairs for supper.

My most vivid memory of that house is of washed nappies drying on the fire and of babies on my parents' laps crying for milk. A year after the move my mother gave birth for the sixth time, to twins. Maria and Natasha were a welcome addition to the family for my mother, who with four sons and only one daughter until then had been very much hoping for girls to help even out the gender ratio. When my mother came back from the hospital she called me downstairs from my room to see my new baby sisters. It was July – the height of summer – and I could tell she was hot because some of the hairs at the front of her brow were stuck to her forehead. My father told me to sit down on the settee in the living room and to keep my back straight. Then, slowly, he collected the babies in his arms and brought them over to me and placed them carefully so that I held one in each arm. I looked down at them; they had fat cheeks and tiny fingers and were dressed in matching pink tops with little plastic buttons. One of the buttons was undone, so I did it up.

The size of our family brought its own set of challenges. Bathtime was always a rushed and crowded affair. Every Sunday evening at six o'clock my father would roll up his sleeves and call the boys (myself and my brothers Lee, Steven and Paul) to the bathroom for our weekly ablutions. I hated bathtime: having to share the bath with my brothers, having hot soapy water poured from a jug over my hair and face, my brothers splashing each other, the heat of the steam that filled the room. I often cried but my parents insisted that I bathe with the others. With so many people in one house, hot water was at a premium.

So, too, was money. With five children under the age of four, my parents both stayed at home to help raise the family. The absence of a wage-earner put a lot of pressure on my mother and my father; arguments over what and where and when to spend became more and more common. Even so, my parents did everything they could to ensure we children were never without such things as food, clothes, books or toys. My mother made bargain hunting in the local charity and second-hand shops and markets into an art, while my father proved himself very handy around the house. Together they made a formidable team.

I stayed away as much as I could manage from the daily hubbub; the bedroom I shared with my brother Lee was where my family knew to find me, no matter what the time of day. Even in summer, when my brothers and sisters were running around together in the sunshine outside, I remained seated on the floor in my room with my legs crossed and my hands in my lap. The carpet was thick and lumpy and clay-red; I often rubbed the back of my hands against its surface because I liked the feel of its texture on my skin. During warm weather the sunlight poured into my room, brightly tingeing the many specks of dust swimming in the air around me as they merged into a single pattern of freckled light. As I sat still and silent for hour after hour, I diligently watched the wash of different hues and colours ebb and flow across the walls and furniture of my room with the day's passage; the flow of time made visual.

Knowing my obsession with numbers, my mother gave me a book of mathematical puzzles for children that she had spotted in a second-hand shop. I remember this was around the time I started primary school, because Mr Thraves – my teacher – told me off if I brought the book into class with me. He thought I spent too much time thinking about numbers and not enough time participating with the rest of the class, and of course he was right.

One of the exercises in the book read like this: There are twenty-seven people in a room and each shakes hands with everyone else. How many handshakes are there altogether?

When I read the exercise I closed my eyes and

imagined two men inside a large bubble, then I imagined a half-bubble stuck to the side of the larger bubble with a third person inside it. The pair in the large bubble shook hands with each other, then each with the third man in the half-bubble. That meant three handshakes for three people. Then I imagined a second half-bubble stuck to the other side of the larger bubble with a fourth person in it. Then the pair in the large bubble needed to each shake hands with him too, and then the half-bubble men shake hands with each other. That would make six handshakes between four people. I continued in this way, imagining two more men in two other half-bubbles, until there were six in all and fifteen handshakes between them. The sequence of handshakes looked like this:

1, 3, 6, 10, 15 . . .

And I realised that they were triangular numbers. These are numbers that can be arranged to form a triangle when you represent them as a series of dots, like so:

Triangular numbers are formed like this: 1+2+3+4+5 . . . where 1+2 = 3 and 1+2+3 = 6 and 1+2+3+4 = 10 etc. You might notice that two consecutive triangular numbers make a square number e.g. $6+10 = 16$ (4×4) and $10+15 = 25$ (5×5). To see this, visually rotate the six so that it fits into the top right corner above the ten.

Having realised that the answer to the handshakes puzzle was a triangular number, I spotted a pattern that would help me to work out the solution. First of all I knew that the first triangular number – one – starts at two people, the fewest needed for one handshake. If the sequence of triangular numbers starts at two people, then the twenty-sixth number in the sequence would coincide with the number of handshakes generated by twenty-seven people shaking hands with each other.

Then I saw that ten, the fourth number in the sequence, has the relationship with four: $4+1 \times 4/2$, and this held for all the numbers in the sequence; for example fifteen, the fifth triangular number, $= 5 + 1 \times 5/2$. So the answer to the puzzle is equivalent to $26+1 \times 26/2 = 27 \times 13 = 351$ handshakes.

I loved doing these puzzles; they stretched me in a way that the maths I was taught in school did not. I spent hours at a time reading and working through the questions, whether in class, the playground or my room at home. Within its pages I found a sense of both calm and pleasure and for a while the book and I became inseparable.

One of the greatest sources of frustration for my parents was my obsessive collecting of different things, such as the shiny, brown conkers that fell in autumn in large quantities from huge trees that dotted a long road near our house. Trees were a source of fascination for me from as far back as I could remember; I loved rubbing the palms of my hands into the coarse, wrinkled bark and pressing the tips of my fingers along its furrows. The falling leaves formed spirals in the air, like the spirals I saw when I did divisions in my head.

My parents didn't like me to go out on my own, so I collected the conkers with my brother Lee. I didn't mind – he was an extra pair of hands. I scooped each conker up from the ground in my fingers and pressed its smooth, round shape into the hollow of my palm (a habit I have to this day – the tactile sensation acts as a kind of comforter, though nowadays I use coins or marbles). I stuffed my pockets one by one with the conkers until each was bulging full. It was like a compulsion, I just had to collect every conker I could see and put them all together in one place. I pulled my shoes and socks off and filled them with conkers too, walking barefoot back to the house with my hands and arms and pockets crammed full to overflowing.

Back at the house, I poured the conkers out onto the

floor in my room and counted them over and over. My father came up with a plastic bin bag and made me count them into it. I spent hours each day collecting the conkers and bringing them back to my room and the rapidly filling sack in the corner. Eventually my parents, fearful that the weight of amassed conkers might damage the ceiling of the room below mine, took the sack out to the garden. They indulged my obsession, allowing me to continue to play with them in the garden, but I was not to bring them into the house in case I left any on the floor for my baby sisters to choke on. As the months went by, my interest eventually waned and the conkers became mouldy, until finally my parents arranged for them to be taken away to the local tip.

A short time afterwards came an obsessive interest in collecting leaflets, of all different sizes. They were frequently pushed through our letterbox with the local newspaper or the morning's post and I was fascinated by their shiny feel and symmetrical shape (it didn't matter what was being advertised – the text was of no interest to me). My parents were quick to complain of the precariously stacked piles that accumulated in every drawer and on every cupboard shelf in the house, especially as they poured out onto the floor every time a cupboard door was opened. As with the conkers, my leaflet mania gradually faded over time, much to my parents' relief.

When my behaviour was good I was rewarded with

pocket money. For example, if there were leaflets on the floor I was asked to pick them up and put them back in the drawer. In return, my parents gave me small value coins, lots of them, because they knew how much I loved circles. I spent hours painstakingly stacking the coins, one atop another, until they resembled shining, trembling towers each up to several feet in height. My mother always asked for lots of small change at the shops she went to, so that I always had a ready supply of coins for my towers. Sometimes I would build several piles of equal height around me in the shape of a circle and sit in the middle, surrounded on all sides by them, feeling calm and secure inside.

When the Olympic Games came to Seoul in South Korea in September 1988, the many different sights and sounds on the television screen, unlike anything I had seen before, riveted me. With 8,465 participants from 159 countries it was the largest games in history. There were so many extraordinary visuals: of the swimmers pulling at the glistening, foamy water, their goggled heads bobbing rhythmically up and down with every stroke; the sprinters racing down the lanes, their brown, sinewy arms and legs reduced to a blur; gymnasts springing and twisting and somersaulting in the air. I was engrossed by the television Olympic coverage and watched it as much as I could from the living room, no matter the sport or event.

It was a piece of good fortune when my teacher

asked the class to write out an assignment based on the Games in Seoul. I spent the next week cutting and gluing hundreds of photos of the athletes and events from newspapers and magazines onto coloured card-board sheets, my father helping me with the scissors. The choice of how to organise the different cuttings was made by a logic that was entirely visual: athletes dressed in red were pasted onto one sheet, those in yellow were put on another, those in white on a third, and so on. On smaller sheets of lined paper I wrote out in my best handwriting a long list of the names of all the countries I found mentioned in the newspapers with participants in the Games. I also wrote a list of all the different events, including Taekwondo – Korea's national sport – and table tennis, which made its Olympic debut in Seoul. There were also lists of statistics and scores, including event points, race times, records broken and medals won. In the end, there were so many sheets of cuttings and written pages that my father had to hole-punch each one and tie them together with string. On the front cover I drew a picture of the Olympic rings in their colours of blue, yellow, black, green and red. My teacher gave me top marks for the amount of time and effort I had put into the project.

Reading about the many different countries repre-sented at the Olympic Games made me want to learn more about them. I remember borrowing one book from the library that was about different languages from around the world. Inside was a description and illustration of the ancient Phoenician alphabet. It dates from around 1000 BC and is thought to have led to the formation of many of the alphabet systems of the modern world, including Hebrew, Arabic, Greek and Cyrillic. Like Arabic and Hebrew, Phoenician is a consonantal alphabet, containing no symbols for vowel sounds; these had to be deduced from context. Whole words were usually written from right to left. I was fascinated by the distinctive lines and curves of the different letters and even began filling notepad after notepad with long sentences and stories exclusively in the Phoenician script. Using coloured pieces of chalk, I covered the inside walls of our garden shed with my favourite words composed entirely of the Phoenician letters. Below is my name, 'Daniel', in Phoenician:

The following year, when I was ten, an elderly neighbour died and a young family moved into the street. One day my mother answered the door to a small girl with blonde hair, who said she had seen a little girl from our house playing outside (that girl was my sister Claire) and asked whether she could come and play with her. My mother introduced her to my sister and me – she thought it a good opportunity for me to mix with other children in the neighbourhood – and we went over to her house and sat in the porch in her front garden. My sister and the little girl soon became good friends and played together most days in her garden. Her name was Heidi and she was around six or seven. Her mother was Finnish, but her father was from Scotland so Heidi had been raised speaking English and was only now beginning to learn her first Finnish words.

Heidi had several children's books with brightly coloured drawings and the word for the object in Finnish under each. Beneath the drawing of a shiny, red apple was the word *omena* and under another of a shoe appeared the word *kenkä*. Something about the shape and sound of the Finnish words I read and heard was beautiful to me. While my sister and Heidi played together I sat and studied the books, learning the many words. Although they were very different from English words I was able to learn them very quickly and remember them all easily. Whenever I left Heidi's garden I would always turn and say to her, *Hei Hei!* – the Finnish word for 'goodbye!'

That summer I was allowed to walk the short distance to and from school by myself for the first time. The route was lined with row after row of hedges and one afternoon while walking home from class I noticed a tiny, red insect covered in black dots crawling inside one of the hedges. I was fascinated by it, so sat down on the pavement and watched it closely as it climbed over and under the sides of each small leaf and branch, stopping and starting and stopping again at various points along its journey. Its small back was round and shiny and I counted its dots over and over. Passers-by on the street stepped round me, some of them muttering under their breath. I must have been in their way, but at the time I did not think of anything but the ladybird in front of me. Carefully, I put out my finger for it to climb onto, then I ran for home.

I had only previously seen ladybirds in pictures in books, but had read all about them and knew, for example, that they are considered lucky in many cultures because they devour pests (they can eat as many as fifty to sixty aphids in a day) and help protect crops. In mediaeval times, farmers considered their help divine and it's for this reason that they are named after the Virgin Mary. The ladybird's black spots absorb energy from the sun, while its colours help to frighten away potential predators because most of them associate bright colours with poison. They also produce a chemical that tastes and smells horrible so predators won't eat them.

I was very excited by my find and wanted to collect as many ladybirds as I could. My mother saw the little insect in my hand as I came through the front door and told me they were 'clingy' and that I should say, 'ladybird, ladybird, fly away home!', but I didn't say it because I didn't want it to fly away. Upstairs in my room was a plastic tub where I kept my collection of coins. I emptied it, pouring the coins into a mound on the floor, then took the tub and placed the ladybird inside it. Then I went back outside onto the street and spent several hours, until it got too dark to see anymore, looking inside the hedges for other ladybirds. As I found each one, I gently picked it up with my fingertips and placed it with the others in the tub. I had read that ladybirds liked leaves and aphids, so I pulled lots of leaves and some nettles which had aphids on them from the hedges and placed them in the tub with the ladybirds.

When I returned home I took the tub back up to my room and put it on the table next to my bed. I used a needle to pick some holes in the sides of the tub so the ladybirds would have plenty of air and light in their new home, then put a large book over the top of the tub, to prevent them from flying away all over the house. For the next week each day after school I went out and picked more leaves and aphids for the ladybirds and took them back to the tub in my room. I sprayed some of the leaves with water so they wouldn't get thirsty.

In class I talked about the ladybirds ceaselessly until my exasperated teacher, Mr Thraves, asked me to bring them in. The next day I took the tub with me to school and showed my ladybird collection to him and the other children in the class. By that time I had found and placed hundreds of ladybirds in the one tub. He took one look and then asked me to put the tub down on his desk. He gave me a folded piece of paper and asked me to take it to the teacher in the next class. I was gone a few minutes. On my return the tub had disappeared. Mr Thraves, worried that the ladybirds might escape from the tub and fly all over his classroom, had told one of the other children to take it outside and release all the ladybirds. When I realised what had happened, my head felt like it was going to explode. I burst into tears and ran from the class all the way home. I was absolutely distraught and didn't say a word to the teacher for weeks afterwards and became agitated if he even called my name.

At other times Mr Thraves could be exceptionally kind towards me. Whenever I became anxious or distressed in class he would take me to the school's music room to help me calm down. He was a musician and often played the guitar to the children in his lessons. The music room was filled with instruments including cymbals, drums and a piano which were used in the school's various productions throughout the year. He showed me how the different keys on a piano produce different notes and taught me simple tunes to play. I liked visiting the room and being left to sit at the piano and experiment with the keys. I have always loved music, because of its ability to help relieve any anxiety I might be feeling and to make me feel calm and peaceful inside.

Feelings of high anxiety were common for me throughout my time at school. I became upset if a school event in which everyone was expected to take part was announced at short notice, or by changes in the normal routines of the class. Predictability was important to me, a way of feeling in control in a given situation, a way of keeping anxiety at bay, at least temporarily. I was never comfortable at school and rarely felt happy, except when left alone to do my own thing. Headaches and stomach aches were frequent signals of how tense I was during this time. Sometimes it got so bad that I did not even make it into class at all, for example if I arrived a few minutes late and realised the class had already gone to assembly. I was terrified of the idea of walking into the hall by myself and didn't want to wait for all the crowds and noise of the children walking back out together afterwards, so I walked straight back home to my room.

The school's annual sports day was a source of considerable distress. I was never interested in joining in and had zero interest in sport. The day involved crowds of shouting onlookers for events such as the sack and egg and spoon races, and the combination of crowds and noise (and quite often summer heat) was too much for me. My parents often allowed me to stay at home rather than risk me having a meltdown. If I felt overwhelmed by a situation I could go very red in the face and hit the side of my head very hard until it hurt a lot. I would feel such a sense of tension within me that I just had to do something, anything, to let it out.

This happened once during a science lesson where Mr Thraves had helped one of the pupils to prepare an experiment involving a ball of play-dough suspended on a piece of string. I was fascinated by this unusual sight and – unaware that it was part of an ongoing experiment – walked over to it and started to touch and pull the dough with my fingers. At this point my teacher became annoyed that I had interfered for no reason (at least as he understood it) and told me off, but I had no idea why he was angry with me and became very confused and upset. I ran from the class, slamming the door behind me with such force that the glass window shattered into pieces. I can still remember hearing the gasps of the children behind me as I ran from the room. When I got home my parents explained to me that I had to try very hard not to react in such a way again. They had to pay a visit to the headmaster, write a letter of apology and agree to pay for the cost of replacing the broken window.

One idea my parents had to help me cope better with my emotions was to teach me how to skip rope. They hoped it would improve my coordination skills and encourage me to spend more time outdoors, outside my room. Though it took some getting used to, I was soon able to skip for long periods of time during which I felt a lot better and calmer within myself. As I skipped I would count each turn and visualise the number's shape and texture as I imagined it to be.

I often found it confusing when we were given arithmetic worksheets in class with the different numbers printed identically in black. To me, it seemed that the sheets were covered in errors. I couldn't figure out, for example, why eight was not larger than six, or why nine wasn't printed in blue instead of black. I theorised that the school had printed too many nines in their previous worksheets and had run out of the right colour ink. When I wrote my answers on the paper the teacher complained that my writing was too uneven and messy. I was told to write every number the same as the others. I didn't like having to write the numbers down wrong. None of the other children seemed to mind. It was only in my teens that I realised that my experience of numbers was very different to that of the other children.

I always completed all my sums well ahead of the other children in the class. Over time, I had progressed, literally, textbooks ahead of everyone else. After finishing, I was asked to sit at my desk and to be quiet so as not to disturb the others while they did their work. I would put my head in my hands and think about numbers. Sometimes while absorbed in my thoughts I would hum softly to myself without realising I was doing so until the teacher came up to my desk, when I would realise and stop.

To fill the time I created my own codes, substituting letters for numbers, so for example: '24 1 79 5 3 62' would encrypt the word 'Daniel'. Here, I paired the letters of the alphabet: (ab), (cd), (ef), (gh), (ij), etc. and gave each pair a number from 1–13: (ab)=1, (cd)=2, (ef)=3, (gh)=4, (ij)=5, etc. Then it was only necessary to distinguish between each letter in the pair. I did this by adding a random number if I wanted the second letter in each pair, otherwise I would simply write the number that corresponded with the pair in which the letter was in. So '24' meant the second letter in the second pair, 'd', while '1' stood for the first letter in the first letter pair, 'a'.

Having first asked the permission of the teacher, I often took the maths textbooks home with me after school. I'd lie on my stomach on the floor of my room with the books spread out in front of me and do sums for hours. One time, my brother Lee was in the room watching me. Knowing that I loved multiplying a number by itself, he gave me some to try, checking the answers with a calculator: '23? 529' '48? 2304' '95? 9025'. Then he gave me a much bigger sum: '82 × 82 × 82 × 82?' I thought for about ten seconds, my hands clenching tight and my head filling with shapes, colours and textures. '45,212,176' I replied. My brother didn't say anything, so I looked up at him. His face looked different; he was smiling. Lee and I hadn't been close up to that point. It was the first time I had ever seen him smile at me.

In my final summer at Dorothy Barley, the teachers organised a week-long trip for several classes, including mine, to Trewern, a residential outdoor centre situated in countryside on the border between England and Wales. My parents believed it would be a good opportunity for me to experience a different environment for several days. A long, shiny coach with a driver who smelled of tobacco came to collect the children and teachers. My father had helped me to pack my clothes and books for the trip and came to see me off.

At the centre, the children were split up into small groups and each group was allocated a hut to stay in for the week. Each hut had just enough room for bunk beds, a sink and a table and chair. I hated being away from home, because everything was mixed up and I find it hard to cope with lots of change. We were expected to wake up very early – around five o'clock each morning – for a run around the field in a t-shirt and shorts. I became very hungry all the time because the centre did not seem to have any of the food I ate at home, such as Weetabix or peanut butter sandwiches. I also had little time to myself, as the children were expected to take part in group activities every day.

One of these was pony trekking, an activity run by the local stable. The day consisted of being shown how to control a pony and then going for a trek around the local lanes, accompanied by a guide. I found it very hard to keep my balance on the pony and kept slipping in the saddle, so I held the reins very tight to stop myself from falling off. One of the stable-owners saw me and became very angry and shouted at me. She was very passionate about her animals, but I didn't understand at the time what I had done wrong and became very upset. After that, I withdrew more and more, spending as much time as possible on my own in the hut.

There were other group activities, including walking in an underground cave. It was dark everywhere so everyone had to wear hats with lights on them. The cave was cold and wet and slimy and I was glad to walk back out onto a log bridge running over a stream. As I made my way slowly over it, one of the boys in the group ran over, laughing, and pushed me hard so I fell into the water. In shock, I fell silent for a long time and just sat in the shallow water, my clothes soaking wet and clinging to my skin. Then I climbed out and walked back to my hut on my own, my face bright red, trying my hardest not to cry from the sudden loss of control. Bullying was sometimes a problem for me because I was different and a loner. Some of the children would call me names or tease me for not having any friends. Fortunately they would always get bored and walk away because I wouldn't fight with them. Such experiences reinforced the perception that I was an outsider and did not belong.

There was one bright spot in the week at Trewern – at its conclusion, workers at the centre awarded various prizes for achievement to the different groups; mine won the award for the cleanest hut.

It was always good to be home. It was where I felt safe and calm. There was only one other place that made me feel the same way – the local library. Ever since I had been able to read I had made my parents take me on a daily trip to the little brick building with graffiti on its walls, and inside, a room with shelf after shelf of colour coded, plastic covered children's books and brightly coloured bean bag seats in the corner. I visited the library every day after class and during the school holidays, no matter the weather, and would stay for hours, often until closing time. The library teemed with quiet and order that always gave me a sense of contentment. The encyclopaedias were my preferred reading material, though they were very heavy to hold so it was necessary to sit at a table with one laid out in front of me. I loved learning different facts and figures, such as the names of the world's capital cities, and making lists of the names and dates of the kings and queens of England and the presidents of the United States of America and other trivia. The librarians became very familiar with my daily appearances and would chat with my parents while I read. The head librarian was sufficiently impressed by my attendance to nominate me for an award, which I subsequently won, recognising effort and achievement in reading. The town's mayor awarded the prize – appropriately enough, a book token – in a short ceremony at the town hall. As I went to collect my prize the mayor bent over and asked me my name, but I didn't hear him and said nothing because I was too busy counting the links on his mayoral chain, and I am not very good at doing more than one thing at a time.

5

Odd One Out

I remember standing alone under the shade of the trees that dotted the perimeter of the school playground, watching the other children running and shouting and playing from the sidelines. I am ten and know that I am different to them in a way that I cannot express or comprehend. The children are noisy and move quickly, bumping and pushing into one another. I'm constantly afraid of being hit by one of the balls that are frequently thrown or kicked through the air, which is one of the reasons why I prefer to stand on the edges of the playground far away from my schoolmates. I do this every playtime without fail, so that it soon becomes

a running joke and it is perceived as common knowledge that Daniel talks to the trees and that he is weird.

Actually I never talked to trees. It is pointless to talk
to things that cannot answer you. I talk to my cats, but
that is because they can at least answer with a meow. I
liked spending time among the playground's trees
because there I could walk up and down, absorbed
in my thoughts, and not worry about being pushed or
knocked over. As I walked, it felt for brief moments as
though I could make myself disappear by standing
behind each tree. There was certainly no shortage of
times when I felt like I wanted to vanish. I just did not
seem to fit in anywhere, as though I had been born into
the wrong world. The sense of never feeling quite
comfortable or secure, of always being somehow apart
and separate, weighed heavily on me.

I was gradually becoming more and more aware of
my loneliness and began to long for a friend. All my
classmates had at least one and most had several. I
would spend hours at night awake in bed looking up at
the ceiling and imagining what it might be like to be
friends with somebody. I was sure it would somehow
make me less different. Perhaps then, I thought, the
other children will not think I'm so strange. It did not
help that my younger brother and sister had several
friends who sometimes came home with them from
school. I would sit by the window overlooking the
garden and listen to them playing. I could not understand why they weren't talking to each other about

really interesting things, like coins or conkers or numbers or ladybirds.

Sometimes other children in the class would try to talk to me. I say 'try' because it was difficult for me to interact with them. For one thing, I did not know what to do or say. I almost always looked down at the floor as I spoke and did not think to try to make eye contact. If I did look up, I would look at the other person's mouth as it moved while they were speaking. Sometimes a teacher speaking to me would ask me to look him in the eye. Then I would bring my head up and look at him, but it took a lot of willpower and felt strange and uncomfortable. When I talked to someone, it was often in a long, unbroken sequence of words. The idea of pausing or of taking turns in a conversation just did not occur to me.

I was never purposefully impolite; I did not understand that the purpose of conversation was anything other than to talk about the things that most interested you. I would talk, in very great detail, until I had emptied myself of everything that I wanted to say and felt that I might burst if I was interrupted in mid-flow. It never occurred to me that the topic I was talking about might not be of interest to the other person. I also never noticed if the listener began to fidget or look around, and would carry on talking until I was told something like: 'I have to go now.'

Listening to other people is not easy for me. When someone is speaking to me it often feels like I'm trying to tune into a particular radio station and a lot of what is said just passes in and out of my head like static. Over time, I have learned to pick out enough to understand most of what is being talked about, but it can be problematic when I am being asked a question and I don't hear it. Then the questioner can sometimes get annoyed with me, which makes me feel bad.

Conversations in the class or in the playground were regularly impeded by my inability to stay 'on topic'. I often found my mind wandering, in part because I remember so much of what I see and read and a chance word or name in the middle of a conversation can cause a flood of associations in my mind, like a domino effect. Today, when I hear the name 'Ian' a mental picture of someone I know with this name comes spontaneously into my head, without me having to think about it at all. Then the picture jumps to the Mini he drives, which in turn causes me to picture various scenes from the classic film *The Italian Job*. The sequence of my thoughts is not always logical, but often comes together by a form of visual association. At school, these associative detours sometimes meant I stopped listening to what was being said to me and teachers often told me off for not listening or not concentrating enough.

Sometimes I am able to hear every word and pick out every detail that is being said to me, yet still not respond appropriately. Someone might say to me: 'I was writing an essay on my computer when I accidentally hit the wrong button and deleted everything' and I will hear that he hit a button he was not supposed to and that he was writing an essay as he hit the button, but I won't connect the different statements and get the overall picture – that the essay was deleted. It is like joining the dots in a children's colouring book and seeing every dot but not what they create when joined together. I find it almost impossible to 'read between the lines'.

Just as difficult for me is to know when to respond to statements that are not phrased explicitly as questions. I tend to accept what is said to me as information, which means that I find it hard to use language socially as most people do. If a person says to you: 'I'm not having a good day', I have learned that the speaker expects you to say something like: 'Oh, really', and then to ask what it is that is causing the bad day. I would get into trouble in class if a teacher thought I was being unresponsive, when in fact I had not realised that they were expecting me to give an answer. For example, he would say: 'seven times nine' while looking at me, and of course I knew that the answer was sixty-three, but I did not realise that I was expected to say the answer out loud to the class. It was only when the teacher repeated his question explicitly as: 'What is seven times nine?' that I gave the answer. Knowing when someone expects you to reply to a statement is just not intuitive for me, and my ability to do things like converse socially has only emerged as the result of lots of practice.

Practising such things was important to me, because

more than anything else I wanted to be normal and to have friends like all the other children. Whenever I mastered a new skill, such as keeping eye contact, it felt so positive because it was something that I had had to work very hard on and the ensuing personal sense of achievement was always incredible.

I had to get used to the feeling of loneliness that hung around me in the playground. Aside from my walks among the trees, I spent my time there counting stones and the numbers on the hopscotch grid. I often became entirely wrapped up in my own thoughts, oblivious to what others around me saw or thought. When I felt excited by something I would cup my hands together close to my face and press my fingers against my lips. Sometimes my hands would flap together and make clapping sounds. If I did this at home, my mother would get upset and tell me to stop. But I wasn't doing it deliberately – it just happened – and many times I did not even realise I was doing it until someone pointed it out to me.

The same was true when I talked to myself. A lot of the time I did not even realise I was doing it. I sometimes find it very hard to think my thoughts and not say them out loud. Whenever I am absorbed in my thoughts there is a lot of intensity involved and this affects my body; I can feel it tense. To this day I cannot stop my hands moving around and pulling unconsciously at my lips as I think to myself. When I talk to myself, it helps me to calm down or to focus on something.

Some of the boys in the playground would come up to me and tease me by mimicking my hand flapping and calling me names. I did not like it when they came up very close to me and I could feel their breath on my skin. Then I would sit down on the hard, concrete ground and put my hands on my ears and wait for them to go away. When I felt very stressed I counted the powers of two, like this: 2, 4, 8, 16, 32 . . . 1024, 2048, 4096, 8192 . . . 131072, 262144 . . . 1048576. The numbers formed visual patterns in my head that reassured me. Since I was so different, the boys weren't entirely sure how to tease me and soon tired of it when I did not react as they wanted me to, by crying or running away. The name-calling continued, but I learned to ignore it and it did not bother me too much.

People with Asperger's syndrome do want to make friends, but find it very difficult to do so. The keen sense of isolation was something I felt very deeply and was very painful for me. As a way of compensating for the lack of friends, I created my own to accompany me on my walks around the trees in the playground. There is one that I remember very clearly to this day and when I close my eyes I can still see her face – wizened, yet beautiful, at least to me. She was a very tall woman, more than six feet in height, and covered from head to toe in a long blue cloak. Her face was very thin and creased with wrinkles, because she was very, very old – more than a hundred years of age. Her eyes were like narrow, watery slits and they were often closed as if she were in deep thought. I didn't ask where she came from; it didn't matter to me. Her name, she told me, was Anne.

Every playtime was spent in long, thoughtful conversations with Anne. Her voice was soft and always kind, gentle and reassuring. I felt calm being with her. Her personal history was a complex one: she had been married to a man called John who had worked as a blacksmith. They had been happy together but had had no children. John had died long ago and Anne was alone and was as grateful for the companionship as I was. I felt very close to her, because there was nothing I could say or do that would make her dislike me or want to leave me. I could unburden myself of all my thoughts and she would stand and listen patiently, never interrupting me or telling me how strange or weird I was.

A lot of the time conversations that we shared were philosophical, about life and death and everything in between. We talked about my love of ladybirds and my coin towers, about books, about numbers, about tall trees and the giants and princesses of my favourite fairy tales. Sometimes I would ask Anne a question that she would not answer. Once I asked her why I was so different from the other children but she shook her head and said that she could not say. I worried that the answer was terrible and that she was trying to protect me, and so I didn't ask her again. Instead she told me not to worry about the other boys and that I would be fine. A lot of what she said to me was meant as reassurance and it always worked, because when I left her I always felt happy and peaceful inside.

One day she appeared as I walked as usual behind the trees, kicking my heels against the thick, scabrous bark as I went, and she stood very still, in a way that I had not seen before. She asked me to look at her because what she had to say was important. It was difficult for me to look her in the eye, but I pulled my head up and looked at her. Her mouth was clamped tight closed and her face was softer and brighter than the few occasions that I had seen it before close up. She did not say anything for several minutes and then she spoke very, very softly and slowly and told me that she had to go and could not return. I became very upset and asked her why, and she told me that she was dying and was here to say goodbye. Then she disappeared for the last time. I cried and cried until I couldn't cry any more, and I continued to grieve for her for many days afterwards. She was very special to me and I know I will never forget her.

Looking back, Anne was the personification of my feelings of loneliness and uncertainty. She was a product of that part of me that wanted to engage with my limitations and begin to break free from them. In letting go of her, I was making the painful decision to try to find my way in the wider world and to live in it.

* * *

While other children went out onto the streets and parks to play after school, I was content to stay in my room at home, sit on the floor and absorb myself in my thoughts. Some of the time I played a simple form of solitaire of my own creation, with a deck of cards in which each card was given a numerical value: ace as 1, jack 11, queen 12, king 13, while the numbers on the other cards determined their values. The object of the game is to keep as many cards as possible. At the start, the deck is shuffled and then four cards are played onto a pile. If, after the first card, the total value of the cards in the pile is at any point a prime number, then those cards are lost. This is where, like many other forms of solitaire, an element of luck comes in. Imagine that the first four cards are: 2, 7, king (13), 4. This pile is safe so far, as 2+7=9 which is not prime and 9+13 is 22 which is not prime and 22+4=26 which is also not a prime number. The player now decides whether to risk putting another card onto the pile or to start a new pile from scratch. If the player decides not to risk a new card on the pile then the cards from the pile are safe and are retained. If the player plays a new card and the total reaches a prime number at any point then the whole pile of cards is lost and a new pile is started. The game ends when all fifty-two cards in the deck have been played into piles, some lost and some successfully held. The player counts up the total number of safely retained cards to work out his final score.

I found this game fascinating to play, because it involves maths and memory at the same time. Once the player has a pile of four cards that have not yet totalled a prime number, the decision of whether or not to continue with that pile or to start a new one is dependent on two factors: the total value of the cards at that point, and the values of the remaining cards in the deck. For example, if the first four cards are as in the earlier example: 2, 7, 13 (king) and 4=26, then the player must first consider how many possible primes could be 'hit' with the next card if the pile is continued. The next primes after 26 are 29, 31 and 37 (because the highest value card is 13, the king, there is no need to consider numbers higher than 39 in this example). So a 3, 5 or jack (11) would lose the pile, but any other card would allow it to grow safely.

Remembering the values of the remaining cards in the deck also helps the player. For example, if you were to reach a total of 70 from ten cards with three cards in the deck remaining, it is obviously an advantage to know that they are, say, a 3, a 6 and a 9. In such a situation, the player should keep the ten cards and start a new pile because 73 and 79 are both prime. I remembered the values of all the cards remaining in the deck at any given point in the game in this way: there are four of each type of card in a deck (four aces, four 2s etc.) I visualised each set of four cards as a square composed of dots. The squares had different colours or textures, depending on the card value; for example, I would see the set of four aces as a brilliant, bright square, because I always see the number one as a very bright light. I see the number six as a tiny, black dot so I would see the set of four 6s as a square-shaped black hole. As the game is played and each card is turned up, the different squares in my head would change shape. When the first ace in the deck appears, the bright square changes to a bright triangle. With the first 6, the black square becomes a black triangle. At the time that the deck produces the second ace the bright triangle becomes a bright line and with the third ace, a bright dot. As all four of each card value are played out from the deck the shape in my head for that set of cards would disappear.

The cards help to illustrate a particular quality of prime numbers – their irregular distribution. In the game, certain total values for a pile are better than others. For example, a total of 44 is better than a total of 34 because from 44 the player can only hit two primes – 47 and 53 – whereas from 34 it is possible to hit four primes: 37, 41, 43 and 47; twice as many. A total value of 100 for a pile is particularly unfortunate as it is possible to hit five primes with the next card: 101, 103, 107, 109 and 113 (with an ace, 3, 7, 9 and king respectively).

My parents were always concerned that I spent too much time alone in my room and did not make any effort to play with the other children in the street. My mother was friendly with a woman who lived several houses down and who had a daughter about my age.

One day she took me with her to visit and to sit and talk with the girl while the women chatted over tea. Whenever I began to talk about the things that interested me, the girl would interrupt, and this made me feel very angry because I could not get the words in my head out, and it felt as though I was unable to breathe. Then I started to become very red in the face, which made her laugh. This only made me redder and redder, and suddenly I got very upset and I stood up and hit her and she began to cry. Not surprisingly, I was not invited back.

So my mother encouraged my brother Lee to let me join in when he went out to play with his friends. His best friend was a boy called Eddie who lived two streets away. Most of the time my brother and Eddie would play in Eddie's garden – he had many more toys than we had and they enjoyed playing ping pong or football together while I sat on the swing and rocked myself rhythmically back and forth.

In the summer Lee would go with Eddie's family for a week's holiday to the coast. My mother suggested that I go along with them and Eddie's mother was more than happy for me to do so. I was hesitant, because I did not like the idea of being away from home. But my mother was very keen for me to go, hoping that it would help me to feel more confident around people. After a lot of gentle but persistent persuasion, I agreed to go.

Once we arrived, it seemed that everything would be

fine. The weather was warm and clear and Eddie's family were very kind and thoughtful towards me. But after only a day away from home I felt a crushing sense of homesickness and wanted to speak to my mother. There was a payphone near where we were staying so I took the coins I had in my pocket and rang home. My mother answered to hear me crying into the receiver. She asked what was wrong, but I could only reply that I did not feel right here and wanted to come home. After several minutes my credit was almost gone and I asked her to ring me back, then put the phone down and waited. I did not realise that she could not have known the number of the phone to call unless I had given it to her; I had just assumed that she would know it. I waited and waited and waited, standing by the phone for more than an hour before finally walking away. The rest of the holiday went by in a blur of tears. Eddie's mother was frustrated and annoyed that I would not join in with them, but spent most of my time on my own in the room where the family slept, sitting on the floor with my hands over my ears. It was my first and last holiday with Eddie and his family.

For much of my childhood, my brothers and sisters were my friends. Even when they could throw and catch better than me, and make friends at school long before I could, they loved me because I was their big brother and I could read them stories. They learned, over time, to engage me by doing things together that they knew I would enjoy and could fully participate in.

After watching my mother doing some ironing, I pulled all the clothes that I had from the drawers and cupboards in my room and took them downstairs to the living room. My mother agreed to give me the iron once it was switched off and had cooled, then I proceeded to take each piece of clothing and rub the iron over it. My brothers and sisters were watching me and asked if they could play with me. I had seen my mother spraying some of the clothes with water before ironing them, so I told my sister Claire to take the spray and use it for each item of clothing, then pass the item on to me. My brother Lee wanted to join in too, so I told him to stand on the other side of me, take the clothes after I had rubbed them over with the iron, and fold each item up. I told my brother Steven, who was four at the time, to then put each of the clothes into a pile: one for t-shirts, one for jumpers, another for trousers and so on. Once we had run out of clothes, Steven was told to unfold everything and pass it back to Claire who would re-spray the items before passing them on to me to iron again, and I would pass them on to Lee to fold and he would pass them back to Steven to re-sort into piles – and round and round it went. We often played for hours at a time.

Another game I played with my brothers and sisters involved me collecting every book I could find from around the house – hundreds of them – and putting them in the largest bedroom, which was the girls' room. There I would sort through each book, dividing them into piles of fiction and non-fiction, then sub-dividing these piles by topic: history, romance, trivia, adventure . . . Then I put each of the divided piles of books into alphabetical order. I cut sheets of paper into small squares and wrote out tickets for each book by hand, listing its title, name of author, year of publication and category (non-fiction>history>'D'). I put the books into boxes, with all the books in the correct order, and positioned them around the room for my brothers and sisters to browse and read. Whenever one of them wanted to take a book from the room, I would take the ticket out and put it in a jar and give them another piece of paper with a time on it for them to return the book by. During the summer holidays my parents allowed us to keep the books together in the boxes with their tickets, though at other times we had to remove all the tickets at the end of the game and help to put the books back on the different shelves and tables around the house.

Sometimes when I played with my brothers and sisters I would walk over to them and touch their necks with my index finger because I liked the sensation, which was warm and reassuring. I had no sense that what I was doing was annoying to them or socially inappropriate and it was only when my mother told me so that I stopped, though occasionally I would still touch a person's neck if I became very excited and the sense of touch was a way for me to communicate that excitement to those around me. I found it difficult to understand the concept that people had their own personal space that was not to be entered and that had to be respected at all times. I had no idea that my behaviour could be irritating and intrusive and felt hurt when a brother or sister became angry with me for what I considered to be no reason.

There were lots of things that I found difficult, like brushing my teeth. The scratchy noise of teeth being brushed was physically painful to me, and when I walked past the bathroom I would have to put my hands over my ears and wait for the noise to stop before I could do anything else. Because of this extreme sensitivity I brushed my teeth only for short periods and then often only with the intervention of my parents. I was very fortunate that I rarely had toothache, probably in large part because I drank lots of milk and did not eat much sugary food. The problem continued for several years and led to frequent arguments with my parents who could not understand why I would not brush my teeth without them having to compel me and often brought the toothbrush and paste into my room, not leaving until I had used them. It was not until the start of puberty that I realised that I had to find a way of brushing my teeth regularly. In particular, my brothers and sisters and the children at school were noticing that my teeth were discoloured and teased me about it, which made me more and more reluctant to even open my mouth to talk because of the insults that would ensue. Eventually I tried putting cotton wool into my ears so that I could not hear the noise as I brushed my teeth. I also watched the small television that I had in my room at the same time to take my mind off the fact that I was using the toothbrush; otherwise it would make me gag. Together these small efforts helped me to clean my teeth from day to day. On my first visit to the dentist in many years I used cotton wool in my ears to help block out the sounds of the drill and other equipment. Nowadays I am able to brush my teeth twice each day without difficulty. I use an electric toothbrush, which doesn't produce the painful scratchy noise that manual brushing does.

Learning how to tie my shoelaces was just as much of a problem for me. However hard I tried, I just could not get my hands to perform the manoeuvres shown to me over and over again by my parents. Eventually my mother bought me a toy – a large Mother Hubbard boot with thick, coarse shoelaces – to help me practise. I spent many hours practising, often until my hands were red and itching from prolonged contact with the boot's laces. In the meantime, my father did my shoes up for me every morning before taking me to school. I was eight before I finally mastered my laces.

Then there was the problem of telling left from right (something I have to concentrate to remember to this day). Not only did my father have to tie my laces until I was eight, he also had to put my shoes on for me first. Sometimes I got frustrated when I tried to put the shoes on myself and would throw them in the heat of a tantrum. My parents had the idea of putting labels – marked 'L' and 'R' – on each shoe. It worked and I was then finally able to put my shoes on by myself and to understand simple directions a lot better than before.

When I walked, even out on the street, I always kept my head firmly down and watched my feet as they moved. Often I would bump into things and suddenly stop walking. My mother walked with me and kept trying to remind me to bring my head up, but even when I did it would quickly fall back down again. Eventually, she asked me to pick out a point – a fence or a tree or a building – in the distance and to keep watching it as I walked. This simple idea helped me to keep my head up, and over the following months my coordination improved a lot; I stopped walking into things and my confidence grew.

For the Christmas just before my ninth birthday I was given a bicycle as a present, as was my brother Lee. My parents put stabilisers on both bikes, though my brother was able to take his off very quickly whereas mine remained on for many months, even though Lee was more than two years younger than me. I had poor balance and coordination and found it hard to steer and pedal at the same time. I practised by sitting on a chair in the kitchen, holding a long wooden spoon in front of me while trying to move my feet in circles against the legs of the chair. With enough practice, I was able to ride with my brother around the streets close to our home. He would race me, going much too fast, so that I would panic and stumble. Falling off the bike was something I quickly got used to, along with the many scratches and bruises on my hands and legs.

My poor coordination also made learning how to swim a slow and frustrating process; I was the last child in my class to be able to swim even a width of the pool. I was frightened of the water, of being pulled under and of not being able to return to the surface. The pool instructors were sympathetic and gave me armbands and foam blocks to help me float safely, but my difficulty only helped to reinforce the sense that I was different and separate from my peers, who could all swim seemingly effortlessly years before I was finally able to make my first strokes. Only as I approached puberty did I finally and suddenly lose my fear of being in the water and found that I could float and move by myself, without my armbands. The sense of exhilaration was enormous and it felt as though I had taken a huge step forward. My body was finally beginning to do the things that I wanted it to.

It was in my final year at primary school that a new addition came to the class, an Iranian boy called Babak whose parents had fled the Khomeini regime. Babak was intelligent, spoke fluent English and was very good at maths. In him I finally found my first real friend. He was the first person to make any real attempt to look past the things that made me different and instead focus on what we had in common: our love of words and numbers in particular. His family was always very kind to me too – I remember his mother giving me cups of tea to drink while I sat with him in his garden and played Scrabble.

Babak had lots of confidence and he got on well with everyone in the class. It came as no surprise when he was picked to play the lead role in the school's ambitious production of *Sweeney Todd*, a gruesome story of a murderous barber whose victims are used to make meat pies. Babak attended rehearsals every day for several weeks and invited me along to watch. I sat on the costume box in the corner, out of sight, and read the lines of dialogue as they were spoken. I attended each and every rehearsal with him. Then on the day of the production, Babak did not appear for the final rehearsal; he was ill and unable to come in. The teachers began to panic and asked if anyone else could fill his role. I realised that from my serial attendance of the rehearsals I had learned every word of the story, and nervously agreed to take part. Come the evening of the performance I recited all the sentences for the character in the correct order, only occasionally missing my place because I found it difficult to listen to the other people on stage and could not easily judge which lines were for the audience and which were for dialogue between the different actors. My parents, who were in the audience, later said I did not show much emotion and kept looking down at the floor, but I had made it to the end at least and that was success enough for them and for me.

6

Adolescence

I counted the seven seconds that it took my father to stagger and slump to the living room floor, falling into his own shadow. The sound of his breathing as he lay on his back was coarse and dingy, and his eyes looking up into mine were round and staring and bloodshot.

My father's illness had been presaged in the gradual changes in his behaviour following the birth of my twin sisters. He had stopped working in the garden and refused to see old friends. He swung between long periods of talkativeness and others of almost complete silence. Physically, he seemed to age ten years in the space of a few months: he lost a lot of weight and became very thin, moving increasingly slowly and tentatively around the house. Even the lines and creases in his face grew deeper.

I was ten when I became an accidental witness to my father's first mental breakdown. In the months leading up to it, my mother had done all that she could to protect us from the sights and sounds of his erratic decline. On this day, however, I had walked unnoticed into the living room and found him stumbling around the room, his eyes wide and bulging, muttering unintelligibly to himself. I didn't do anything except watch him in silence, unsure of how to feel, but at the same time not wanting to leave him alone. The noise of my father's fall brought my mother quickly inside and she gently pulled me away and told me to go upstairs to my room. She explained that he was unwell and that she was waiting for a doctor to call. Ten minutes later an ambulance arrived, its sirens switched off. I watched from the top of the stairs as my father was put onto a stretcher, wrapped in a blanket and carried away by the paramedics.

The next day the house was quieter and felt colder somehow too. I remember sitting in my room and trying to think through my feelings for my father, because I knew that I should be feeling something but I didn't know what. In the end I realised that the home felt incomplete without him and I wanted him to return.

We were told that my father needed time to rest and

had been taken to a hospital where he could get better. He was away from home for several weeks, during which time we children were not allowed to see him, though my mother travelled by bus to visit. The hospital was a long-stay psychiatric institution, but we were too young to know what mental illness was. My mother did not discuss my father's condition with any of us and would only say that he was getting better and would be home soon. In the meantime, with seven children (five of them four years of age or younger) to care for, my mother relied heavily on the support of her parents and family friends and helpers brought in from social services. My brother and I were also expected to help out as much as possible, tidying and drying dishes and carrying shopping.

When my father came home from his hospitalisation, there was no celebration. Instead, there was an attempt at some sort of return to normality, with my father trying to do those everyday things – changing nappies and cooking supper – that had been the core of his daily routine before his illness had struck. But things were different and I think I knew even then that they would never be the same again. The man who had protected and cared for me with all his strength and energy had gone and had been replaced with one who needed protecting and caring for himself. He was prescribed medication and advised to rest regularly by the doctors at the hospital, and every day after lunch he went up to his room and slept for several hours. My mother asked my brothers and sisters to play quietly, as quietly as I did, so as not to disturb my father's rest. Whenever one or both of the babies started to cry, my mother would rush to take them out of the house to the garden before attending to them.

The relationship between my parents changed too. My mother, who had previously relied heavily on my father both practically and emotionally, now had to reimagine their life together and in a sense start all over again. Their conversations became short and the co-operation between them, which they had previously perfected, seemed to have been lost. It was as if they had to relearn their relationship. They argued more and more frequently and their voices grew loud and dark and I didn't like to hear them argue, so I put my hands over my ears. Often after a particularly loud argument my mother would come upstairs and sit with me in the quietness of my room. I wanted to wrap the soft silence around her like a blanket.

The state of my father's health fluctuated from day to day and from week to week. There were long periods of time when he might talk and behave as before, only to be interrupted by sudden spells of disjointed, repetitive speech, of confusion and isolation from the family. He was hospitalised on several more occasions over the following years, each for weeks at a time. And then, just as suddenly as his illness had first appeared, my father seemed to make a recovery of sorts – he began to eat and sleep a lot better, grew physically and emotionally stronger and regained his confidence and initiative. My parents' relationship improved and there followed the birth of an eighth child, my sister Anna-Marie, in the summer of 1990. Seventeen months later came my parents' final child, Shelley, born four days before my thirteenth birthday.

The improvement in my father's condition and the continued growth in family numbers meant another move, in 1991, to a four-bedroom house in Marston Avenue. It was terraced, situated close to shops and a park, with a large garden at the back. Like all the houses before it, it had only one bathroom and toilet for the entire family of eleven. Queues outside the bathroom door were a frequent sight. The living and dining rooms were separated by a set of doors, which were often kept unlocked so that the rooms downstairs flowed into one another. Whenever I had some thought or idea in my head I would walk through the rooms, living room to dining room to kitchen to corridor back to living room, in a continuous circuit round and round with my head down and my arms fixed by my sides, absorbed in my thoughts and totally oblivious to anyone around me.

I started secondary school in September 1990. That summer, my mother took me into the town centre to buy my first school uniform: a black blazer and trousers, white shirt and black and red striped tie. My father tried to teach me how to put a tie on, but after repeated attempts I was still no nearer to being able to do it by myself, so he suggested that I simply loosen and re-wear the same knot through the week. I fidgeted a lot as I tried my uniform on – the blazer was made of a thick fabric and felt heavy on, and the new black leather shoes were tight-fitting and squeezed my toes. I also had to have a bag to take the various books into school, and an assortment of classroom equipment: pens, pencils, notepad, sharpener, eraser, compass, ruler, protractor and sketchbook.

The school was Barking Abbey (nearby is the church of St Margaret where Captain James Cook married in 1762). My first day there started with my father helping to knot my tie and do up the buttons of my shirt cuffs. We travelled by bus to the school gates, where he told me to be brave, that the first day at a new school is always a big challenge and that I should try to enjoy it. I watched him as he walked away, until he had disappeared from view. Then, hesitantly, I followed the other children being led into the nearby gymnastic hall where the headmaster was due to address the new pupils. The hall was just large enough for all the children to sit down on the floor, with several teachers standing against the walls. The floor was dusty as I sat down at the back just as the headmaster – Mr Maxwell – asked for silence and began to speak. I found it difficult to concentrate and listen to what he was saying, so I looked down at the floor, rubbed the tips of my fingers through the light dust and waited for the assembly to end. We were assigned class numbers and the name of our form tutor and asked to proceed quietly to our classrooms. I was excited to discover that my class was next door to the school library. After registration, we were given a timetable for the week's lessons. Each subject was taught by a different teacher in different classrooms in various parts of the school. Moving from one hour to the next, from subject to subject, classroom to classroom and teacher to teacher was one of the hardest things for me to adapt to in the transition from primary to secondary school.

There were few familiar faces in my form class from my old school, Dorothy Barley. Babak, my one good friend from there, had gone on to another school in a different part of town. I felt extremely nervous and did not speak to anyone in my new class, not even to introduce myself. Instead, I kept looking at the clock and wanting the hands to rotate faster and faster and bring the day to a close. With the noisy ringing of the bell, the children piled out into the playground. I hung behind, waiting for the other children to leave, afraid of being pushed or jostled as they scrambled out of the room. I walked next door to the library, pulled an encyclopaedia from the reference shelves and sat at a table alone and read. I timed myself using the library's clock on the wall, as I did not want to be late for the return to class. The thought of walking in and seeing the children already sitting, all looking up at me, was terrifying to me. When the bell for lunch rang I made the short walk to the library once more and read at the same table.

At primary school I had eaten packed lunches prepared the night before by my mother. However my parents were now keen for me to eat my lunch at school, because coming from a low-income family I qualified for vouchers against the cost of the meal. After a half hour of reading I made my way round to the entrance of the dining hall. The queues had dissipated and I was able to take a tray up to the counter on my own and select the food I wanted. I pointed to the fish fingers, chips and beans. I was hungry, so I put a doughnut from the dessert section on to my tray. I walked over to the till and handed my voucher to the woman as she pressed the various buttons. The voucher was not enough to include the doughnut and she told me that I would have to pay the extra. I had not expected this to happen, felt myself redden and became very anxious, feeling as though I would burst into tears at any moment. Noticing my distress, the woman told me not to worry as it was my first day at the school, and to keep the doughnut. I found an unoccupied table and sat down. The hall was half-empty but I ate my food as quickly as possible, before anyone could come and sit at the table with me, and then left.

At home time, I waited for the scrum of children to pour out into the streets before making my way to the bus stop I recognised, because it was the one that I had got off at that morning. It was the first time I had ever had to use public transport by myself and I did not realise that I had to get on the bus going in the other direction for it to take me towards home. When the bus arrived I climbed on and stated my destination, something I had rehearsed over and over again in my mind. The driver said something but I did not hear him clearly and automatically put my money out for the ticket. He repeated what he had just said, but I could not process the words in my head because I was concentrating so hard on not panicking at being aboard a bus alone. I stood there until finally the driver sighed loudly and took the money. I pulled off the ticket and sat in the nearest empty seat. As the bus moved off I waited for it to turn around at any moment to go in the direction of home, but it did not and carried on taking me further and further from where I wanted to go. I became anxious and ran over to the door and waited impatiently for the bus to stop and the doors to open. Realising my mistake, I jumped off and walked across the road to another bus stop. This time, when the bus arrived and I gave the driver the name of my destination he did not say anything other than to state the price for the ticket, which I already knew, and I was relieved to be on the right bus – even more so when, twenty minutes later, I saw my street from the bus window and knew I had returned home safely at last.

With time and experience, I was able to travel alone by bus to and from school. It was a short walk from the house in Marston Avenue to the bus stop and, as I could remember all the times from the bus timetable, I was never late except, of course, when the bus itself was late.

Each school day began with registration in the form class, followed by the lessons scheduled for that day in different rooms and buildings around the school grounds. Unfortunately, since I haven't any natural instinct for direction, I get lost very easily, even in areas I have lived in for many years, except for routes that I have specially learned by sheer repetition. The answer for me was to follow my fellow pupils to each of the lessons.

Maths was naturally one of my favourite subjects at school. On the opening day of term, each pupil had had to complete a maths test from which they were graded according to ability and allocated a place in sets one (the highest), two, three or four. I was placed in set one. From my first experience in the class I noticed that the lessons moved much more quickly than those in primary school. Everyone in the classroom seemed engaged and interested and there were a wide range of topics taught. My favourites among them were numerical sequences such as the Fibonacci (1, 1, 2, 3, 5, 8, 13, 21, 34, 55 . . .) where each new term in the series is derived from the sum of the two preceding, data handling (such as calculating the mean and median of a set of numbers) and probability problems.

Probability is something that many people find unintuitive. For example, the answer to the problem

'A woman has two children, one of whom is a girl. What is the probability that the other child is also a girl?' is not 1 in 2, but 1 in 3. This is because, knowing that the woman already has a girl and therefore cannot have two boys, the remaining possibilities are: BG (boy and girl), GB (girl and boy) and GG (girl and girl).

The 'Three Cards Problem' is another example of a probability question producing an apparently counter-intuitive solution. Imagine there are three cards: one is red on both sides, one is white on both sides, and the third is red on one side and white on the other. A person puts the cards into a bag and randomly mixes them together, before pulling one out and putting it face up on the table. A red side is showing – what is the probability that the other side is also red? Some versions of this problem point out that as there are only two cards with red sides, one with a second red side and the other with a white side, the odds would appear to be 1 in 2, i.e. the other side of the card is equally likely to be red or white. However, the actual probability that the other side of the card is also red is 2 in 3. To picture this, imagine writing the letter 'A' on one side of the card with two red sides, and 'B' on its other side. On the card with one red side and one white side, imagine writing the letter 'C' on its red side. Now consider the situation where a card is drawn showing a red side. The possibilities are that it is red sides 'A', 'B' or 'C'. If 'A', the other side is 'B' (red), if 'B' the other side is 'A' (red) and if 'C', the other side is white.

Therefore the odds of a red side under the one showing are 2 in 3.

Another favourite subject at secondary school was History. Since I was very small I have loved learning lists of information and my history class was full of them: lists of names and dates of monarchs, presidents, and prime ministers were of particular interest to me. I much prefer non-fiction to fiction, so reading about and studying many different facts and figures from key events in history was immensely enjoyable for me. I also had to analyse texts and attempt to understand the relationships between different ideas and historical situations. I was enthralled by the notion that a single, seemingly solitary event could lead to a sequence of many other events, like a row of dominoes. History's complexity fascinated me.

From the age of eleven, I began to create my own world of historical figures, such as presidents and prime ministers, and imagined complete and intricate biographies for every one of them. The various names and dates and events would often just come to me and I spent a lot of time thinking through the invented facts and statistics of each. Some are influenced by my knowledge of real historical people and events, while others are very different. I continue even to this day to ponder my own historical chronologies and to add to them with new individuals and events over time. Below is an example of one of my created historical figures:

Howard Sandum (1888–1967),
32nd president of the United States of America

Sandum was born to a very poor family in the Mid-West and fought in the First World War before being elected as a Republican to the House of Representatives in 1921 and to the Senate three years later, aged just thirty-six. He became a state governor in 1930 and was elected President of the United States in November 1938, defeating sixty-four-year-old Democrat incumbent Evan Kramer. Sandum served as wartime president, declaring war on Nazi Germany and Japan in December 1941. He was defeated by Democrat William Griffin (born 1890) in November 1944 (presidential elections occurring every six years) and subsequently retired from national politics. Sandum wrote his memoirs in retirement – they were published in 1963. Sandum's only child, his son Charles (1920–2000), followed his father into politics, serving as a congressman from 1966–1986.

There were school subjects that I really hated and struggled in. Woodwork, for example, was one that I found boring and couldn't apply myself to at all. My classmates were happy enough to cut and sand and construct with various pieces of wood, but I found it difficult to follow the teacher's instructions and often lagged behind everyone else in the class. Sometimes the teacher became impatient with me and came over and worked the equipment for me. He thought I was being lazy, but the truth was that I felt in a totally alien environment and I didn't want to be there.

The same was true of Physical Education. I enjoyed activities that didn't require interaction with others – trampolining and high jump were activities I really liked and looked forward to. Unfortunately, most lessons were spent on the field playing games such as rugby and football that required lots of teamwork. I always dreaded the moment when team captains were picked. They then selected their team mates one by one until there was only one person left standing on their own – that person was almost always me. It was not that I could not run fast or kick a ball in a straight line. I just could not interact with the other players on the team; I didn't know when to move and when to pass and when to let someone else take over. During a match there was so much noise around me that I would switch off without realising it, and not know what was going on around me until one of the players or the coach came and stood over me and told me to 'pay attention' or 'get involved'.

Even as I got older, I still found it very difficult to socialise with my classmates and make friends. In the first months after starting secondary school I was fortunate to meet Rehan, a British Asian whose family had moved to the UK from India fifty years before. Rehan was tall and skinny with very thick, black hair that he combed frequently with a brush he kept in his schoolbag. The other pupils at the school teased him because of his unusual appearance – his two front teeth were missing and his upper lip was scarred from a childhood accident. Perhaps because he too was shy and nervous and – like Babak – something of an outsider, we became friends and spent a lot of time together. Rehan was the person I would always sit next to in class and the one I would walk around the school corridors with, talking about things that interested me, while the other children played in the field and playground outside at breaktime. Sometimes Rehan would recite poetry to me; he read a lot of poetry, wrote his own poems and was very interested in words and language. It was something else that we had in common.

Rehan loved London and travelled regularly around it on the Underground, frequenting historical parts where famous poets had once lived and worked, and visiting his mosque in Wimbledon for Friday prayers. He was surprised to discover that though I had lived in London all my life I had hardly seen any of it apart from the streets around my family home. So, at weekends, Rehan would occasionally arrange to take me with him on his travels on the Underground to see such attractions as the Tower of London, Big Ben and Buckingham Palace. He would buy my ticket for me and walk with me down to the platform where we waited for the train. It was gloomy and humid and I

remember looking down at my feet and noticing a
burned out match and a crumpled cigarette packet
with the words: 'Warning: Smoking can seriously
damage your health' on it.

As we sat together on the train, Rehan showed me
the map of the different Underground lines and
stations: yellow for the Circle line, blue for the Victoria
line, green for the District line. The train shook a lot as
it travelled, as though it was sneezing continuously. I
did not like central London – it was full of people and
noise and different smells and sights and sounds – and
there was too much information for me to mentally
organise and it made my head hurt. It helped that
Rehan took me to quiet sites away from the crowds
of tourists and sightseers: museums, libraries and
galleries. I liked Rehan a lot and felt safe whenever
I was with him.

Throughout secondary school, Rehan was often ill
and was increasingly away from class. I gradually had
to learn to cope without his company while at school,
which was not easy and I became vulnerable to my
classmates teasing me over having no friends at all.
When the school library was closed, I spent break-
times walking round and round the corridors by myself
until the bell rang for the next class. I dreaded group
activities in the classroom, where previously I would
have worked happily with Rehan. Instead the teacher
would have to ask in a loud voice: 'Who can do me a
favour and team up with Daniel?' No one would want

to, and I often had to work on my own which suited me fine.

My father taught me how to play chess when I was thirteen. One day he showed me the chessboard and pieces that he used when he played with friends and asked if I wanted to learn. I nodded, so he demonstrated how each of the pieces moved on the board and explained the basic rules of the game. My father was self-taught and only played occasionally to pass the time. Even so, it was a surprise to him when I beat him in our first game together. 'Beginner's luck,' he said and put the pieces back in their starting positions and we played another game. Again, I won. At this point my father had the idea that I might benefit from playing socially at a chess club. He knew of one nearby and told me he would take me to play there the following week.

There are many mathematical problems involving chess; the most famous and my personal favourite is known as the 'Knight's Tour', which is a sequence of moves by a knight chess piece (which moves in an 'L' shape – two squares vertically and one horizontally or one square vertically and two horizontally) where each square of the board is visited just once. Many famous mathematicians have studied this problem over the centuries. A simple solution uses the 'Warnsdorff Rule', according to which at each step the knight must move to the square that has the lowest degree (the degree of a square is the number of squares to which the knight can move from that square). Below is an example of a successfully completed Knight's Tour:

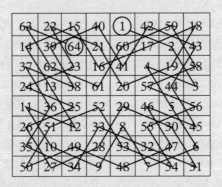

The club I played at was a twenty-minute walk from my home. My father took me each week and collected me at the end of the evening. The club met at a small hall next to a library and was run by a short man called Brian, who had a wrinkled face like a prune. Inside the hall were sets of tables and chairs and elderly men sat hunched over chessboards. It was very quiet while the games were being played, except for the noise of pieces being moved and clocks ticking and shoes tapping and the hall's fluorescent lights humming. My father introduced me to Brian and told him that I was a beginner who was very shy but keen to learn and enjoyed playing the game. I was asked if I knew how to assemble the board at the start of a game. I nodded and was asked to sit at an empty table with a chessboard and a box of pieces, and to take each piece and put it on the correct initial position on the board. Once

I had finished, Brian called an elderly man with thick glasses over to sit opposite me and play a game with me. Brian and my father both stood back and watched as I nervously moved each piece until a half hour later my opponent pushed his king over and stood up. I didn't know what this meant until Brian came over and said simply: 'Well done – you won.'

I liked going to the club each week to play. It wasn't noisy and I did not have to talk or interact very much with the other players. When I wasn't playing chess at the club, I was reading about it at home in books I had borrowed from the local library. Soon, all I could talk about was chess – I even told people that I wanted to be a professional chess player when I got older. When Brian asked me if I wanted to play competitively for the club against players from other clubs in the area I was excited, because it meant I could play even more chess, and I agreed straight away. Matches took place on different days of the week, but each player in the team was asked ahead of time if they were available to play. Brian would collect me in his car and drive me, sometimes with another member of the team, to the evening's venue. These games were played more formally than those at the club and each player had to write down the game's moves as they were played on a sheet of paper provided before the start of play. I won most of my games and so quickly became a regular member of the club's match team.

After each match, I would take my sheet of paper

home with me and replay the moves on my own chessboard while sitting on the floor of my bedroom, analysing the positions reached to try and find ways of improving. It was advice I had read in one of my chess books and it helped me to avoid repeating mistakes and to become familiar with various common positions during a game.

The hardest part of playing chess for me was trying to maintain a deep level of concentration over a long game that could often last two or three hours. I tend to think deeply in short and intense bursts, followed by longer periods when my ability to concentrate on something is much reduced and less consistent. I also find it hard to switch off from small things happening around me and this affects my concentration: someone exhaling noisily across the room from me, for example. There were games where I would play myself into an advantageous position and then lose my concentration, play a weak move or series of moves and end up losing. That was always very frustrating for me.

Each month I read the latest chess magazine at my local library. In one issue I read an advert for an upcoming tournament not far from my home. It read in part, 'Entry Fee: In advance – £5 off. On the day – £20'. I tend to read things very literally, and I was not at all sure what 'off' meant here and guessed that it was an abbreviation of 'offer'. I asked my parents if I could participate and they agreed and gave me a postal order for the amount I thought I needed to send: £5. Two weeks later I arrived at the hall where the competition was being held and gave my name. The man looked through his notes, and then said that I must have misunderstood because I still owed an additional £15 (because I was paying on the day, I had to pay the full fee). Fortunately, I had some extra money with me and paid, still feeling very confused about the whole situation.

The games were timed and I started my first match confidently and played quickly. Soon I had a strong position on the board and a big time advantage against my opponent as well. I was feeling very positive. Then suddenly my opponent made his move, pressed the button on the clock and stood up quickly. I watched him as he paced up and down the hall while he waited for me to respond. I had not expected him to do this and found that I could not concentrate well while he walked up and down, his shoes squeaking on the hard, shiny floor. Totally distracted, I played a series of poor moves and lost the game. I felt thoroughly disappointed, but also unable to go on with the other games because I just could not get my concentration back. I walked out of the hall and went home, deciding that tournament play was not for me.

I continued to play regularly by myself with a chess set on the floor of my bedroom. My family knew not to disturb me when I was in the middle of a game. When playing by myself, chess was soothing, with its fixed and consistent rules and repeated patterns of pieces and positions. At sixteen I created a game of 18 moves and sent it to the chess magazine I read avidly on my regular library visits. To my surprise, it was published several months later as the lead item in the issue's letters pages. My parents were so proud that they had the page framed and hung it on my bedroom wall.

Earlier that same year, 1995, I sat my GCSE exams, scoring the highest possible grade – A$\star$ – in History, A grades in English Language and English Literature, French and German, two B grades in the sciences and a C grade in woodwork. In my preliminary maths exam I had scored an A, but in my final exam I was given a B grade because my algebra was relatively poor. I found it very difficult to use equations that substituted numbers – to which I had a synaesthetic and emotional response – for letters, to which I had none. It was because of this that I decided not to continue maths at Advanced level, but chose to study History, French and German instead.

One of my A-level French teachers, Mrs Cooper, helped to organise my first overseas trip to Nantes, a coastal city on the banks of the Loire river in north-western France, when I was seventeen. The teacher knew a family there who was happy to accommodate and look after me during my stay. I had never needed a passport before and had to arrange one at short notice before flying over in the middle of summer. I remember feeling very anxious about leaving my family, about flying on an aeroplane and about going to another country. But I was also very excited about having the opportunity to use my French and I coped well. Over the ten-day holiday I was treated extremely well by the family, given my own space when I needed it, and encouraged all the time to use and practise my French. Every conversation was *en français* – during games of table tennis, trips to the beach and over long and lazy seafood meals. I returned home unscathed, except for the sunburn suffered by my sensitive skin.

That same summer, a German boy called Jens came to our school to study to help improve his English. As I was the only student in my form class who could speak German he sat with me during lessons and walked with me wherever I went. I liked having someone to talk to and spend time with during breaks and we conversed in a mixture of German and English. Jens taught me many modern German words, such as *Handy* for 'mobile phone' and *Glotze* for 'TV set', which I had not read or heard before. After he returned to Germany we stayed in touch by email; he writes to me in English and I reply in German.

Adolescence was changing me – I was growing taller and my voice deeper. My parents taught me how to use deodorant and how to shave, though I found it very difficult and uncomfortable and let my stubble grow very long a lot of the time. The rush of hormones was also affecting the way I saw and felt about the people around me. I did not understand emotions; they were things that just happened to me, often seemingly appearing from nowhere. All I knew is that I wanted to be close to someone, and not understanding closeness as being primarily emotional, I would walk up to some of the other students in the playground and stand very close to them until I could feel the warmth of their body heat against my skin. I still had no concept of personal space, that what I was doing made other people feel uncomfortable around me.

From the age of eleven I knew that I was attracted to other boys, although it would be several years before I considered myself 'gay'. The other boys in my class were interested in girls and talked a lot about them, but it did not make me feel any more of an outsider – I was already more than aware that my world was very different to theirs. I never felt shame or embarrassment about the feelings that I had, because I did not consciously choose to have them; they were as spontaneous and real as the other physiological changes of puberty. All throughout my teens my confidence was always very low because of the teasing I received and my inability to talk and interact comfortably with my peers, so dating was never a possibility for me. Although there were sex education classes at school, they never interested me and did not address the feelings that I was experiencing.

I had my first crush at sixteen, after entering the sixth form at school. My form class was much smaller than before with only a dozen students, and among the new intake was a boy who had recently moved to the area and was studying History at A-level, as I was. He was tall and confident and sociable, in spite of being new to the school – in many ways he was the total opposite to me. Just to look at him made me feel strange: my mouth would go dry and my stomach churn and my heart beat very fast inside my chest. At first it was enough for me to see him each day at school, though if he was late arriving to class I would be unable to concentrate on the lesson, waiting for him to walk through the door.

One day I saw him reading in the school library and sat down at the table next to him. I was so nervous that I forgot to introduce myself. Fortunately he recognised me from class and just went on reading. I sat there, unable to speak, for fifteen minutes, until the bell rang for the end of break and he stood up and walked away. Then I had the idea that if I helped him with his history coursework, it would be a lot easier for me to interact with him. I wrote out page after page of notes for the past month's history lessons and gave them to him when I next saw him in the library. He was surprised and asked why I had done this for him. I answered that I wanted to help him because he was new to the school. He took the notes and thanked me. I wrote other notes for him, which he accepted only after I reassured him that it had been no trouble for me. However, there was never a moment in which he spoke to me as a friend or made any effort to spend time with me. I soon felt restless and wrote about how I felt in a short note that I gave him one break time in the library. I walked out of the room as soon as I had handed him my message, unable to stay while he read my innermost thoughts. Later, at the end of the school day, as I walked towards the gates I saw him standing in the middle of the path, watching and waiting. Deep down I wanted to turn and run, still feeling unable to face him, but it was too late; he had already seen me. We stood together on the path and for a brief, happy moment it seemed as though he had entered my world. He handed me back my note and said simply and gently that he could not be the person that I wanted him to be. He was not angry or upset and did not rush away, but stood patiently looking at me until I dropped my head and walked away.

Back home, I did what I always did in such moments of sadness and uncertainty – I listened to my favourite music, which always seemed to help soothe me. My favourite band was The Carpenters, but I also listened intently to other musicians as well, such as Alison Moyet and The Beach Boys. I have a very high tolerance for repetition and sometimes played the same song a hundred times over on my Walkman, listening in an unbroken sequence for hours at a time.

My two years in sixth form were difficult for other reasons too. The change in how the lessons were structured and the subjects studied came as a shock to me and I found it hard to adapt well. In my history class, the themes that I had studied for the past two years were replaced with unrelated ones that I had no interest in at all. The amount of written work required also increased considerably and I struggled to write more about events and ideas that I knew and cared much less about. At the same time, however, the relationship I had with my history teacher, Mr Sexton, was very good, much better than with any of my peers. He respected my love for the subject and enjoyed talking with me after class about those areas that I was most interested in. The extra flexibility at A-level also meant that I could study at my own pace much more than before and the classes were smaller and more focused. By the end of the final term, however, I felt exhausted and unhappy. Though I performed well in my final exams, it did not help me to answer the question that by this time I was asking myself continuously: 'What now?'

7

Ticket to Kaunas

My parents always expected that I would go to university. They supported me steadfastly throughout my studies and were proud of my academic success. Both my mother and father had left school without qualifications and no one in the family had previously gone into higher education. But I was never comfortable with the idea of going on to university. Though I had worked hard at improving my social skills, I still felt awkward and uncomfortable around people. I had also had enough of the classroom and wanted to do something new and challenging. However, like many people at eighteen, I had no clear idea yet of what that might be. When I told my mother that I had decided not to go on to university she told me she was disappointed. At the time my parents were not sure that I would be able to fully adapt to the demands of the outside world. After all, I still found that the smallest things – like brushing my teeth and shaving – required a great deal of time and effort.

Every day I read the back pages of the newspaper, looking at various job adverts. At school I had told the careers officer that I wanted to be a postal sorter or a librarian one day. The idea of working in a sorting office, putting each letter in exactly the right slot, or in a library, surrounded by words and numbers, in environments that were structured, logical and quiet, had always seemed ideal to me. But the libraries in my area were not looking for new staff and some required particular qualifications that I did not have. Then I saw a small newspaper advert asking for individuals interested in doing volunteer work overseas. I had read so much in books about the different countries of the world – I knew the names of all the capital cities of Europe – that the idea of living and working in a different country far away struck me at once as both a terrifying and enormously exciting prospect. It was a huge step to even contemplate, but I knew that I did not want to live with my parents forever.

I talked it over with my family. They were not sure, but said it would be okay for me to call the number in the advert for more information. A few days later some leaflets came through the door. The people who had placed the advert represented a youth branch of VSO – Voluntary Services Overseas – an international development charity and the largest volunteer-sending organisation in the world. They were particularly looking to provide young people from deprived areas of the UK with an opportunity – to perform volunteer work in another country – that would otherwise not be available to them. Successful applicants would be sent to positions in parts of Eastern Europe and would be given ongoing training and support throughout the duration of their placement. After further conversations with my family I filled out the application form and waited to hear from the organisers.

I felt very anxious about the possibility of leaving my family and travelling hundreds of miles away to a new life in a new country. But I was an adult now and knew that I had to do something if I was ever going to be able to make my own way in the world outside my room at home. My German friend Jens had encouraged me to travel, as he had done to Britain. He believed the experience would make me more confident and open to other people. I certainly hoped that by travelling overseas I would find out much more about myself, about the sort of person I was.

A letter arrived telling me that my application had been accepted and that I would need to attend an interview in central London. On the day, my parents gave me the money for a taxi so I would be sure not to be late. My father helped me with the knot in my tie and I wore a new shirt and trousers. The labels in the shirt kept rubbing against my back and I scratched and scratched until it felt very red and sore. Once I arrived at the building I went up in an elevator – watching the numbers as they flashed up on the little screen above the door – and then reached the reception and gave my name. The lady flicked through some pages then made a tick with a purple ink pen and asked me to take a seat. I knew that what she meant was 'please sit down' and not to pick up one of the seats in the waiting area and take it with me, so I walked over and sat and waited.

The waiting area was small and dark because the only windows were too small and set too high up in the walls to let in much light or air. The carpet was faded and there were yellow crumbs on the patch near my chair where someone had eaten a biscuit while waiting to be called in. There were magazines with lots of creases in them in a small pile on a table in the middle of the room, but I did not feel like reading so I looked down at the floor and counted the crumbs. Suddenly a door opened and I heard a voice calling my name. I stood up and walked over to the office, careful not to knock the magazines over as I passed them. The office itself had a large window and was much brighter. The woman behind the desk shook my hand and asked me to sit down. She also had lots of sheets of paper. Then the question came that I had most expected: What makes you think you would make a good volunteer? I looked down and took a deep breath and remembered what my mother had said about emphasising the positive. 'I can think very carefully about a situation, I can understand and respect difference in others and I am a quick learner.'

More questions followed, such as whether I had a partner I would miss if posted overseas (I did not) and if I considered myself a tolerant person of other countries and cultures (I did). The interviewer asked me what I would like to do as a volunteer, what kind of work I was best at doing. I answered that I had sometimes helped younger students at school with their foreign language class work, and that I would enjoy teaching English. The woman smiled and wrote something down. Then she asked if I knew anything about Eastern Europe and I nodded and said that I had studied the history of the Soviet Union at school and knew the names and capital cities of all the different countries. Then she interrupted and asked if I would mind living in a much poorer country. I became silent for a few moments because I do not like being interrupted, but then I looked up and said that I would not mind and would bring the things that I really needed, like books and clothes and music cassettes to listen to, with me.

At the end of the interview the woman rose from her chair, shook my hand and told me I would be informed of their decision soon. After arriving home my mother asked me how the interview had gone but I did not know what to say because I had no idea. Several weeks later I received a letter in the post telling me that I had passed the interview stage and was required to attend a week of training the following month at a retreat centre in the Midlands. I was excited to have passed the interview, but very anxious too because I had never travelled on a train on my own before. There was a sheet of paper with the letter that gave directions to the centre for those coming by train and I memorised them word for word to reassure myself. When the first morning of the week arrived, my parents helped me finish packing and my father travelled with me to the train station and stood with me in the queue for the ticket. He made sure I got on at the right platform and waved me goodbye as I boarded.

It was a hot summer's day and inside the train felt airless and uncomfortable. I quickly sat in a window seat that had no one nearby and put my bag on the floor and squeezed it tight between my legs. The seat felt spongy and no matter how much I fidgeted I could not sit comfortably. I did not like being on the train. It was dirty, with plastic sweet wrappers on the floor and a crumpled newspaper on the empty seat in front of me. As the train moved it made a lot of noise, which made it hard for me to concentrate on other things, like counting the scratches in the windowpane next to me. Gradually the train filled with people as it travelled between stations, and I became more and more anxious as the stream of commuters sitting and standing around me grew in numbers. The cacophony of different noises – magazine pages being flicked and Walkmans playing loud, thudding music and people coughing and sneezing and talking noisily – made me feel unwell and I pressed my fingers into my ears when it felt as though my head was about to shatter into a thousand pieces.

It was not a moment too soon when the train eventually reached my destination and the sense of relief I felt was palpable. But with my poor sense of direction I worried that I would end up getting terribly lost. Luckily I spotted a waiting taxi, climbed inside and gave the address to the driver. The short ride brought me to a large red and white building, dotted with windows and surrounded by trees, with a sign that read 'Harborne Hall – Conference and Training Centre'. Inside, an information leaflet told visitors that the hall dated from the eighteenth century and was a former convent. The reception was gloomy with brown wooden pillars reaching up to the ceiling, dark brown leather chairs and a wooden bannister staircase opposite the desk. I was given a name badge to wear at all times while at the centre, as well as a key and the number of my room and a schedule for the week's events.

Upstairs, my room was lighter and felt a lot fresher. There was a small sink in the corner, but toilets and showers were situated down the hall. The thought of having to use shared facilities to wash myself (I showered daily at home) was an unpleasant one for me, and I woke very early each morning during the week to be certain that I was in and out of the bathroom before anyone else was up.

On the first day at the centre I was told that I had been assigned an English-teaching placement in Lithuania. I had only previously heard of the name and that of its capital city – Vilnius – and was given books and leaflets to learn more about the country and its people. There was then a group introduction with a dozen other young people who were going to various volunteer placements across Eastern Europe. We sat in a circle and each of us had a minute to introduce ourselves. I was very nervous and tried not to forget to make eye contact with members of the group as I gave my name and that of the country I was going to. Of the other volunteers that I met, one was an Irishman with long, curly hair who was being posted to Russia. Another, a young woman, had received a placement working with children in Hungary.

There were long periods of unoccupied time that the other volunteers spent socialising in the games room, chatting and playing pool. I preferred to stay in my room and read, or visit the hall's information room, filled with books and charts, and study in quiet. During meal breaks, I would rush down to get my food first and eat it as quickly as I could to avoid having lots of people around me. At the close of each day, I sat alone out on the grass in the secluded grounds outside the hall and stared up at the trees standing tall against the warm, fading colours of the evening sky, absorbed in my thoughts and feelings. There was anxiety, of course, about the trip and whether or not the placement would be successful. But there was something else as well: excitement that I was finally taking charge of my life and my destiny. Such a thought took my breath away.

The training consisted of three parts. The first was designed to encourage teamwork, participation and cooperation. The volunteers were divided into small groups and asked to devise a system between them for removing coloured plastic balls in particular sequences from a filled box given to each team. When I was given simple and clear instructions by my fellow team members I performed well and was happy enough to play my part for the purpose of the exercise. Exercises such as these could sometimes last for several hours, so the biggest challenge for me was to stay focused and maintain my levels of concentration throughout.

There was also a group discussion about cultural values and practices, which was meant to stimulate debate among the volunteers, challenge preconceptions and promote tolerance. At one point, after watching a video together about the exotic types of food eaten in different parts of the world, the discussion leader asked the group how we might feel about a country where people ate a lot of their food smeared in animal fat. Many of the volunteers in the room creased up their faces and said that it sounded disgusting. Realising that he was probably referring to butter (which he was), I replied that I did not mind at all that people ate it.

Towards the end of the week there was a lecture on the countries of Eastern Europe and their geography and social and political situations. The lecture lasted an hour and everyone was expected to take notes. I sat and listened but did not write anything down. At one point the lecturer asked me why I was not making notes and I answered that I could remember everything that he had said and was making the notes mentally, in my head. I had always made notes in this way; it had helped me a lot during my school exams. He asked me several questions in order to test me and I got each one right.

Back at home after the training, I waited to receive final confirmation of the placement in Lithuania. It came by post: a large package of printed notes with maps, names and contact numbers, accommodation and work details and plane ticket. My parents were very nervous for me and worried whether I would be able to cope being away from home for so long, but I was just excited to be taking what I considered to be a big step forward in my life. I could hardly believe it but, at nearly twenty, I was finally moving out, eight hundred miles away.

The republic of Lithuania is one of the three Baltic States, sharing borders with Latvia to the north, Belarus

to the southeast, Poland to the south and the Kalinin-
grad Oblast of Russia to the south-west. In 1940,
during the Second World War, Lithuania was annexed
by the Soviet Union. It later came under German
occupation and fell again to the Soviet Union in
1945. Lithuania was the first Soviet republic to declare
its independence, on Sunday 11 March 1990. Soviet
forces tried to suppress the accession – notably during
an incident at the capital's TV Tower, which resulted
in the deaths of several civilians – but were unsuccess-
ful. In 2004, Lithuania became a full member of
NATO and the European Union.

In the taxi to the airport I watched the other cars
driving past and counted them. My head was pound-
ing and I felt sick. I could not believe that I would not
see my family again until the following year. Before I
left, I promised my mother I would phone home every
week with a progress report and would make sure I was
eating enough. At check-in, it was surprisingly quiet – it
was October and the summer holidays were long over –
and I had little trouble checking my luggage in and
going through security to the departures area. After a
long wait, when I walked up and down over and over
again and made very regular checks of the departures
screen, my flight was finally announced and I ran to the
gate and boarded the plane. It was half empty and I felt
huge relief at having no one sitting next to me. I sunk
into my seat and read the notes I had been sent about
the centre I was being posted to, practising under my

breath the pronunciation of the different names of people and places. I was undisturbed by the attendants during the flight and as the plane came in to land at Vilnius International Airport I checked that I had my camera with me; it was nearing winter and I was looking forward to taking lots of photos of the snow.

At immigration, there were short queues and policemen dressed from head to toe in black, observing the people as they came past. My passport was checked and then stamped in red with the words *Lietuvos Respublika* (Republic of Lithuania) and I was waved through. After collecting my bags, I was met by the volunteers' coordinator for the Baltic States and driven to my apartment in Kaunas, Lithuania's second largest city, which is located in the centre of the country.

The apartment block was made of concrete and metal, with a vegetable garden at the front tended by its elderly occupants who were all in their seventies and eighties. It was a quiet area, away from main roads and traffic. I was introduced to the landlord, a silver-haired man named Jonas, who explained in broken English the rules of the block and how to do such basic things as turn the heating on and off. He gave me his telephone number to ring in case of an emergency. The coordinator confirmed the address of the centre where I was to perform my volunteer work and gave me written directions to reach there by trolley bus. It was a Friday, so I would have the weekend to settle in before starting my first day at work.

Inside, my apartment was surprisingly spacious and consisted of a kitchen, living room, bathroom and bedroom. The interior was decorated in heavy, dark fabrics and was often gloomy on overcast days. The kitchen had an old oven, cupboards and a refrigerator. There were white tiles, some of them chipped, running up the sides of the walls. In the living room there was a large wall-unit with photos and ornaments belonging to Jonas's family. There was also a small table, sofa and television. The bathroom came with a shower and a washing machine, a luxury at the time in Lithuania. My bedroom was a good size, with a large wardrobe, table and chair, bed and telephone. This was to be my home for the next nine months.

I was too nervous to leave the apartment and explore the area outside during that first weekend in Kaunas. Instead, I busied myself by unpacking and working out how to use the various items around my new home. I watched some television and soon realised that many of the programmes were American imports with Lithuanian subtitles. Jonas had left essentials, like milk and bread and cereal, in the kitchen for me. I hadn't ever had to cook for myself before and made do at first with eating lots of sandwiches and bowls of cornflakes. I would soon have to summon up all my courage to make my first journey to the centre.

On Monday morning I woke early, showered and dressed in a thick coat and scarf. It was already very cold, even though winter had not yet arrived. A short

walk from the apartment brought me to the main road.
I had been told in the instructions given to me by the
coordinator that trolley bus tickets could be purchased
at any of the many newspaper stands that were dotted
along Lithuania's larger streets. Having memorised the
contents of the Lithuanian phrasebook that had been
included in my volunteer kit, I asked for *vieną troleibusų
bilietą* (one trolley bus ticket) and was given a small,
rectangular ticket in exchange for a few *litas* (the
Lithuanian currency). The bus crawled up the long,
steep road, stopping almost every minute to let more
and more people aboard. There were men in caps and
heavy fur coats, young women with children under
each arm and small, elderly women with scarf-covered
heads and myriad plastic bags by their feet. With few
seats and little standing space, the bus quickly became
crammed full and I started to feel sick and dizzy,
gasping for air as though I was drowning in a sea of
people. As the bus inched to the next stop I stood up
suddenly from my seat, almost knocking over a man
standing next to it, and with my head down I pushed
and squeezed my way out into the fresh, open air. I was
sweating and trembling and it took several minutes for
me to feel calm again.

I walked the rest of the way up the steep incline of the
Savanorių Prospektas (Volunteer Avenue) to the top
until I reached number one, a tall brown concrete
building. I walked up the two flights of steps and
pressed a button to the side of the door. Suddenly

the door swung open and a short woman wearing lots of make-up and jewellery greeted me in good English: 'Welcome! You must be Daniel. Please come in. How are you liking Lithuania so far?' I answered that I had not seen much of it yet. The woman introduced herself as Liuda, the centre's founder and director.

Liuda's centre was called the *Socialinių Inovacijų Fondas* (Social Innovation Fund), a non-governmental organisation for unemployed and economically at risk women in the community. Many Lithuanians had lost their jobs in the upheaval that followed the country's secession from the Soviet Union and she had had the idea to found an organisation to help women like herself navigate their way in the new economy.

Volunteers did much of the centre's work and were critical to its success. Like me, some were from other countries, both near and far. I prepared the English lessons alongside an American Peace Corps volunteer in his seventies called Neil. He liked to reminisce during coffee breaks, telling me about the house he had built for himself back in the United States and the mobile home he and his wife had bought following his retirement, in which they had travelled to all fifty states in the Union.

The other teacher at the centre was Olga, a Russian woman with curly red hair and tinted glasses. Whenever she spoke I could see her two gold teeth, one in each corner of her mouth. Olga understood that I was feeling anxious about being in such a completely different environment and explained that it was normal to feel homesick and nervous about starting something new. I really appreciated her words.

My main role as a volunteer was in the classroom. The centre provided a few textbooks and worksheets, but otherwise resources were scarce and I was allowed to organise the class's content however I wanted, which suited me very well. The women who attended the classes were all different in age, background and education and there was never more than twelve to a class, which meant that the students knew each other well and the atmosphere of the lessons was always relaxed and friendly. At the beginning, I felt very nervous about standing up in front of my students and directing the lesson, but everyone was very kind and positive towards me and I gradually became more and more comfortable with the role.

It was through these classes that I met the person who would become one of my closest friends, a middle-aged woman called Birutė. She worked as a translator and her English was already good, but she lacked confidence and attended the class for practice. After the lessons she would come up to the front of the class and speak to me, asking me how I was finding life in Lithuania. Once she asked whether I would like a guide to show me around. I had been too nervous to walk around the city by myself and gratefully accepted her offer.

We walked together down Kaunas's main pedestrian walkway, *Laisvės Alėja* (Liberty Avenue), 1,621 metres long and located in the town centre. At one end of the avenue is Saint Michael the Archangel Church, a huge blue-domed and white-pillared building that glittered and glowed in the sunshine. The church was transformed into an art gallery under Soviet rule and only reopened to public worship following Lithuanian independence. On the other side of the avenue Birutė took me to see Kaunas's old town with its cobbled streets and red brick castle, the country's first defensive bastion, which dates from the thirteenth century.

Each day around noon, following morning class, Birutė would wait for me and we would walk together to the local town hall for lunch. Routines such as these helped me to start to settle down into my new life, by giving each day a consistent and predictable shape that I was happy with. The canteen was located downstairs and was dimly lit and never more than half full. The food here was plentiful and inexpensive, including many traditional Lithuanian recipes such as creamy beetroot soup with meat filled rolls. My eating habits had changed a lot since childhood and I was comfortable eating a wide range of different foods. On days when there was no afternoon class, Birutė and I would eat in one of the many restaurants along *Laisvės Aleja*. My favourite meal was Lithuania's national dish, *Cepelinai*, so named because of the resemblance of their shape to Zeppelins. It is made from grated potatoes and ground meat, boiled and served with sour cream.

The friendship that I shared with Birutė grew deeper

and more special over time. She was always patient and understanding with me, willing to listen and full of advice and encouragement. I do not know how I would have survived in Lithuania without her. When several of the women at the centre told me that they needed more English practice but could not afford the extra class fees, I had the idea of holding a weekly English conversation group at my home, which Birutė helped to organise. The women brought biscuits and helped make tea and coffee and then everyone sat in chairs or on the sofa and talked in English about anything and everything. One evening, Birutė brought and showed slides from a holiday she had taken with her family, and the group watched and asked questions and discussed their own travelling experiences.

Frequently the women in my class and at the centre asked whether I had made any friends of my own age. Inga, Liuda's deputy, introduced me to her nephew, who was three years younger than me, and encouraged us to socialise. Peter spoke good English and was rather shy and very polite. We visited the cinema together in town and watched the latest American releases. Whenever the music became too loud, I pressed my fingers into my ears, though he never seemed to notice.

There were other volunteers in the country from the UK and we were encouraged to stay in touch as a support network for one another. One of the volunteers, Vikram, had recently finished studying for a law degree at university before deciding he did not want a career as a lawyer. We did not have much in common – he talked a lot about football and rock music and other things that I had no interest in – and our conversations were often punctuated by long periods of silence, because I sometimes find it hard to sustain a conversation when the topic is not interesting to me as the words just do not come.

Another volunteer working in Lithuania was Denise, a tall, slim Welsh woman in her thirties who was very energetic in everything that she said or did. Denise was staying in Lithuania's capital, Vilnius, and invited the volunteers in Kaunas to come and visit her and see the city up close. We travelled by bus – I sat at the back so as not to be surrounded by the other passengers – on a bumpy hour-long ride to the city centre. Vilnius was very different to Kaunas – the people walked more quickly and there were many new building developments built in shiny glass and metal. Denise's apartment was clean and brightly painted, with wooden floors. The kitchen chairs were made of wood and the tops of their backs were shaped like rolling hills. I liked rubbing my fingers over them – they had a slightly gritty, ticklish texture. We drank tea and ate biscuits and looked at photos Denise had taken during her stay so far. I liked that the other volunteers encouraged me to participate in their conversations and did not seem to judge me for being different. The volunteers each had their own personality and were all very open and friendly with one another.

The most experienced of the volunteers was a British Asian woman called Gurcharan. She had thick, curly dark hair and wore brightly coloured saris. Her apartment was close to mine in Kaunas and she would come over regularly with bags of laundry to use my washing machine. In return, Gurcharan invited me to her apartment to talk and eat together in the evenings after work. The walls of each room were decorated with multi-coloured Indian pictures and the living room table was covered in candles and burning incense sticks. Gurcharan talked rapidly and I sometimes found it difficult to follow what she was saying. She was very open and spoke a lot about her personal life and encouraged me to do the same. I did not have a personal life and so did not know what to say. When she asked me if I had a girlfriend, I shook my head. Then she asked if I had a boyfriend. I must have blushed, because she then asked me if I was gay. The rapid succession of questions felt somewhat overwhelming, like the continuous pitter-patter of rain upon my head, and it was several moments before I answered her. She smiled broadly and asked if I had any gay friends. I shook my head again.

In one of the leaflets given to all the volunteers before flying out was a list of useful telephone numbers, which I kept next to the phone in my apartment. The conversation I had had with Gurcharan prompted me to call one of the numbers, of a group for gay people in Lithuania, and arrange to meet with one of its local members outside the town hall after work the following day. I had become tired of not knowing who I was, of feeling disconnected from a part of me that I had long been aware of. That phone call was one of the biggest decisions of my life and one of the most important too. All through my classes the next day I felt my pulse racing and could not eat anything. Later, walking down the avenue towards the town hall, I could feel myself shaking and I had to try very hard to push away the pressing thought to turn around and run. As I approached, I could see that the person I was due to meet had already arrived and was standing very still, waiting for me. I took a deep breath, walked up and introduced myself. He was tall and thin and wearing a black jacket that matched the colour of his hair.

Vytautas – a common name in Lithuania – was my age and excited to meet someone from Britain. His English was very good because he enjoyed watching American films and television shows. He invited me to visit him and his partner, Žygintas, that weekend at their home and I accepted. Because I did not like to travel on the crowded trolley buses, they collected me in their car and drove to their apartment on the other side of town. Many of the modern things that they had, such as a widescreen television and a CD player, were relatively rare at the time in Lithuanian homes. Žygintas loved British music and had collected many CDs and played some of them for me. Over food, we talked about our lives – Vytautas was a student while Žygintas worked in a dental practice. They had met through the group and had been together for several years. Over the following weeks I visited them regularly to talk about events, eat together and listen to music. It was always dark when I left to go home at the end of an evening and, though Žygintas was worried for my safety and always offered to drive me back, I looked forward to the long walk alone through the silent, empty, moonlit streets.

Gurcharan was excited to hear about my friendship with Vytautas and Žygintas and wanted to meet them. She offered to cook a meal for the four of us at her apartment, and we gratefully accepted. It was a frosty late autumnal evening when we arrived and it took several minutes of removing coats, hats, scarves and gloves before we entered the living-room. Gurcharan was already busy in the adjoining kitchen cooking several dishes simultaneously, the spicy aromas filling the room and whetting our appetites. Any lingering daylight was fading fast and replaced instead with the flickering, warm glow of candles crammed on various shelves and boxes. The table in the centre of the room had already been laid out with plates and cutlery and glasses that twinkled in the candlelight. Wine was poured for the guests and the food piled onto plates to hand around the table. There were numerous curries full of vegetables and meat and more than enough rice for everyone. Gurcharan was as talkative as ever and asked Vytautas and Žygintas all about themselves over supper. I listened as best I could between mouthfuls of the delicious homemade food, but mostly the conversation did not interest me and after I finished eating I picked up a book from a nearby shelf and began to read to myself. I was embarrassed when Gurcharan exclaimed that I was being very impolite; I hadn't any idea that I was being rude. Just then, as Žygintas was finishing his meal, he stopped suddenly and shouted a word in Lithuanian, before repeating it in English for our benefit: 'Mouse, you have a mouse!' He pointed to the kitchen worktop where he had just seen it appear, jump and vanish before his eyes. Gurcharan smiled slightly and said simply: 'Yes, I know.' She had no problem living with a mouse, she explained to us, and had lived with one before, back at her home in the UK. As long as it did not get in the way, she saw no reason to worry about it. I had not ever had the chance to see a mouse at such close range, and was disappointed to have just missed it. The conversation continued as before and this time no one seemed to mind when I returned to my book and read to myself. At the end of the evening, Gurcharan went to give each of us a kiss as we left; I hesitated so she put her hand in mine instead and squeezed it tight. She was aware that I was different and told me she was proud of me because I was willing to take risks.

About a week later, I was in the kitchen of my apartment making sandwiches when I noticed a small smudge move on the tiled wall opposite. As I moved my head closer and looked again I saw that it was an insect that I had never seen before. The next day, at the centre, I asked Birutė about it. 'It's *tarakonas*' she said, then thought for several moments, searching for the English word, 'a cockroach'. The insects are – I soon discovered – a common problem in many of Lithuania's older buildings. My landlord, Jonas, was telephoned and was very apologetic and promised to treat the infestation. However, the whole block required treatment and, as my neighbours were all very elderly, this proved difficult to arrange quickly. In the meantime Jonas gave me a spray to use on any cockroaches that I saw. I did not mind them too much, though I found them distracting if I saw one while trying to listen to a conversation with someone or watch the television. When I told my parents of the problem in one of my regular phone reports home, they were very unhappy and I had to reassure them that my apartment was otherwise clean, that I was completely healthy and that the landlord was working promptly to deal with the problem. It was several weeks before Jonas was able to complete the treatment across the block and even then the cockroaches persisted, though only making the odd appearance from time to time.

Winter came inexorably over the months following my arrival in Lithuania, bringing heavy snowfall and bitterly cold weather throughout the country. Temperatures fell at night to as low as minus thirty degrees in Kaunas. My apartment was not a modern building; it was poorly insulated and very difficult to keep warm. I borrowed a radiator from one of the volunteer workers at the centre who had bought a new one and was happy to loan the spare to me. I put it in my living room while I watched the television or read in the evenings, and later I would carry it into the bedroom to help keep me warm and sleep comfortably. Jonas put draught excluder around the door and windows after Birutė, to whom I had explained the problem with the constant cold, intervened on my behalf. Apart from the severity of the cold, I loved the wintry weather: the crunching sensation of treading through several inches of freshly laid snow on the way to work and the sight of bright, glistening white all around me. At night, I sometimes put on my coat and boots and walked the still streets while the snowflakes tumbled around my head. I would stop under a blazing street lamp and turn my face up towards the falling sky, stretch out my arms and spin round and round in circles.

In December, as Christmas approached, the women at the centre asked me what my plans were for the festive season. I realised that this would be my first Christmas away from my family and understood Christmas to be a special time to be shared with others. One of my coworkers at the centre, Audronė, insisted that I come and spend the holiday with her and her family and I gratefully accepted. In Lithuania, Christmas Eve is much more important than Christmas Day and preparations for it take many hours. The house is cleaned and everyone must bathe and wear clean clothes before the evening meal. Audronė and her husband collected me and drove me to their home in a large apartment block. As they climbed out of the car I noticed that her husband was extremely tall – more than two metres in height. He reminded me of the number nine.

Inside, I met Audronė's son and mother. Everyone was smiling and seemed happy to meet me. The corridor into the living room was long, dark and narrow, but as I walked slowly along it the gloom ebbed away until I was met suddenly by a rush of bright, swimming light and colour. A long table in the middle of the room was covered with a smooth linen cloth with fine hay spread underneath it. I was told that this was to remind us that Jesus was born in a stable and laid in a manger filled with hay. There were twelve different dishes on the table, all meatless (the number represents the twelve apostles). They included salted herring, fish, winter vegetable salad, boiled potatoes, sauerkraut, bread, cranberry pudding and poppy seed milk. Before eating, Audronė's husband took a plate of Christmas wafers and gave one to each person around the table, including myself. He then offered his wafer to Audronė, who broke off a piece and offered her wafer in turn to him. This continued until each person had broken off a piece of each other's wafer. There was no particular order in which each dish had to be eaten, but

I was told that it was customary to at least sample each food. Each symbolised something important for the year ahead: the bread, for example, represented sustenance for the coming months, the potatoes humility. My favourite was the poppy seed milk – *aguonu pienas* in Lithuanian – served with small, round balls of dough. The milk is prepared by grinding the scalded poppy seeds and mixing them with water, sugar or honey, and nuts. During the meal, Audronė explained to me some of the traditional Lithuanian beliefs surrounding Christmas. For example, it is believed that at midnight on Christmas all the water in the streams, rivers, lakes and wells changes to wine, though only for an instant. Another belief is that at midnight animals can speak, though people are discouraged from trying to listen to them. The following day, 25 December, the family took me to a park filled with snow and we walked and talked together by a huge, frozen lake. It had been a Christmas to remember.

One of the most rewarding experiences for me of living in Lithuania was learning the Lithuanian language. When I first told the women at the centre that I wanted to learn to speak Lithuanian they were puzzled: Why did I want to learn such a small and difficult language? It was certainly true that many Lithuanians spoke enough English for me not to have to learn Lithuanian. In fact, none of the other British volunteers, nor Neil the US Peace Corps volunteer, could say more than a few words. It was considered very strange for a foreigner to even want to attempt to learn Lithuanian. Nonetheless, it was the language I heard spoken around me every day and I knew that I would feel more comfortable, more at home, in Lithuania if I could speak with my friends and students and fellow workers at the centre in their own language.

Birutė was more than happy to teach me. She was very proud of her language and enjoyed discussing and speaking it with me. I wrote words down as I learned them to help me visualise and remember them and studied children's books that Birutė's daughters had read when they were younger. Birutė also taught me a popular Lithuanian nursery rhyme:

Mano batai buvo du
Vienas dingo, nerandu.
Aš su vienu batuku
Niekur eiti negaliu!

Which means: 'I had two shoes, one is missing, I cannot find it. With one little shoe, I cannot go anywhere!'

Within a few days of beginning to learn the language, with Birutė's help I was able to build my own sentences, much to her initial surprise, and within a few weeks I was able to converse comfortably with native speakers. It helped a lot that I always asked my colleagues at the centre to speak with me in Lithuanian as much as possible. Everyone I spoke to complimented me on my ability to speak good Lithuanian, including one of my elderly neighbours who was especially amazed that a young Englishman could converse with her in her own language. It was also a benefit on one occasion when I was invited out with the other volunteers for a meal in a restaurant. The waiter did not understand English, much to the volunteers' annoyance, so I translated the order into Lithuanian for him. I did not mind occasionally having to act as an interpreter for the other volunteers, because I found the experience very interesting and another opportunity for me to practise my language skills.

I was even once mistaken for a native Lithuanian. Walking home one day from the centre, a man wanting directions approached me, persisting even when I kept replying in Lithuanian that I did not know the place he was asking directions for. Eventually I stopped and said: '*Atsiprašau, bet tikrai nežinau. Aš nesu Lietuvis. Esu iš Anglijos.*' ('Excuse me, but I really do not know. I am not Lithuanian. I am from England.') His eyes widened and then he apologised and walked away.

By the spring, I had settled firmly into my life in Lithuania. I had gradually developed routines that gave me a sense of calm and security and that helped me cope with change. Early each morning, just before dawn, I woke and pulled on some loose, warm clothes and went for a long walk through the streets to a local park filled with oak trees. The trees were tall, as though reaching up into the sky, and helped make me feel safe as I walked the identical, well-trodden route around them at the start of each day. After returning to my apartment to shower and get dressed for work, I walked up the long, steep road to the centre and sat and drank coffee while the women gossiped together about personal things that did not interest me. Neil had suffered for some months since Christmas with an increasingly painful back, which numerous trips to doctors had not helped. He eventually had to return to the US for treatment. I took over his classes to fill the gap, which meant that I taught English mornings and afternoons most days of the week. There had been other changes too – Birutė's husband had fallen very ill and she had had to stop attending classes to spend time looking after him. At lunchtime I often stayed at the centre and ate sandwiches I had prepared the night before, though occasionally I ate at a local café with Žygintas whose workplace was near the centre. After work I bought frozen fish fingers, bread, cheese and other essentials before walking back home to prepare and eat supper, read and watch television before bed. I didn't mind being on my own more often, though I missed Birutė and hoped I would see her again before long.

In the summer, work at the centre reduced to a trickle as the students went away for long, coastal holidays with their families. Žygintas's family, like many Lithuanians, had a summerhouse in the countryside and invited me to come and visit him. He gave me instructions for a bus that travelled close by the house and said that he would pick me up and drive me the rest of the way once I had reached the agreed meeting point. The bus was old and shaky and very quickly the route took me out of the towns and into long, muddy roads surrounded only by trees and fields. Žygintas had given me a name to look out for but I could not see it anywhere and was too nervous to ask anyone, so I sat and waited and hoped. Eventually the bus reached a stop next to a series of wooden buildings, the first I had seen for half an hour, so I summoned all my courage and stood and explained in Lithuanian that I was lost. The three other passengers just stared at me so I climbed off the bus and counted to myself because I was shaking and did not know what to do. Then the driver came over to me and without saying a word pointed to a timetable. The name Žygintas had given me was not on there. I looked at my watch; I was an hour late for my meeting with him. I walked into the first building and explained the situation in Lithuanian to a woman standing behind a counter. She shook her head and did not say anything. I tried again, repeating myself in Lithuanian but she again shook her head. Then, out of desperation, I tried English. 'Do you have a telephone?' I asked. On the word 'telephone' she suddenly nodded and pointed to a black telephone in the corner. I ran over to it and dialled Žygintas's number. 'Where are you?' he asked and I gave him the name that I saw on the timetable outside. 'How did you get there?' he asked and then, 'wait there, I'll come and collect you.' Half an hour later his car came and we drove to the summerhouse. On the way, Žygintas explained that I had found myself in one of the parts of Lithuania's countryside inhabited by Russian speakers who do not understand Lithuanian. The delay meant my visit to the house was abbreviated, but I met Žygintas's family and was just in time for a barbecue, followed by a swim in the nearby river.

Birutė, too, wanted me to come over and spend some time at her family's summerhouse. She took me to meet her sister who was a poet. Over cups of coffee she recited some of her poems to us and afterwards we walked together along a lake of clear, blue water. The sky was cloudless and the sun shone brightly, its light sparkling on the water's surface like solar flotsam. As the day went on, Birutė asked me to come with her to a point close by where we could sit and watch the sunset. This was our first meeting in several weeks and our last, too, because my volunteer contract had expired and it was time for me to return home. Birutė told me that our friendship had meant a great deal to her, particularly through what had often been difficult times for her. She felt that I had grown a lot in the time that she had known me. I knew it too and had felt for some time that it was not only my day-to-day life that had changed with the decision to come and live in Lithuania; I myself had changed and had been somehow renewed.

As we sat in silence together, looking out towards the sinking summer sun, our hearts were not heavy because we knew that even as one adventure was ending, another was about to begin.

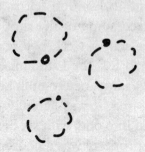

Falling in Love

It's never easy to say goodbye, particularly to a country that has become a home away from home, as Lithuania had for me over the past year. It was July, the height of summer, as I walked up the avenue to the centre for the last time. Inside, Liuda and the other volunteers had gathered in the classroom to see me off. I thanked each of them in Lithuanian for their help and kindness towards me. Liuda presented me with an illustrated leather-bound diary as a farewell gift and told me that she hoped I would fill it with new ideas and future adventures. A part of me was sad to be leaving, but I knew inside that I had achieved everything – personally

as well as professionally – that I could in Lithuania, and
that it was time to move on.

The flight home to London felt as though it might
never end. I passed some of the time by reading and
rereading a letter sent a week before by my parents.
Shortly after I had left for Lithuania, my father had
received news of a large, newly-built house available to
rent in the local area. It was actually two houses that
had been knocked into one, with six bedrooms and two
bathrooms. The property was a godsend to my family,
who moved there not long afterwards. It was to this
new address that I was now returning and the letter
included a photo of the house and directions to it.

A familiar face, my friend Rehan, was waiting for me
at the airport. We had stayed in touch by postcard
throughout my time overseas, but even so it was good
to see him in person after all this time. As he had done
for me years before, Rehan acted as my guide through
the labyrinthine Underground. While we sat together
on the train, he listened patiently to my anecdotes
about my time in the city of Kaunas and asked to
see my photos of the different places and people I had
seen and met. A little while later, he stood up quickly
and told me that we were approaching my stop. There
was just enough time to gather up my bags and thank
him for his company. No sooner had I stepped off the
platform and turned round than the train had pulled
away, its outline rapidly disappearing into the darkness
of a tunnel.

The street outside was completely foreign to me. I walked for a long time before realising that I was stuck: the road's name I'd arrived at wasn't the same as the one in my parents' letter. Perhaps I had taken a wrong turn somewhere. Nervously, I asked a passer-by for help. 'Walk straight on and go right at the next turn,' he said. As I passed the correct road name it suddenly occurred to me how strange it was that I had just had to ask where my own family's street was.

The family were delighted to see me and we spent many happy hours catching up. Some of my brothers and sisters said that I had a slight accent, which was perhaps not surprising as I had been away for so long and had spoken more Lithuanian than English in that time. My mother showed me around the house and my new room, which was situated at the back, away from the road, and was the quietest of all the rooms. It was small, especially after all the space I'd had in Lithuania, though there was still enough space besides a bed for a table and chair and a small television set. I liked the newness of my room; it represented a tangible sense that my return to the UK was a step forward in my life and not back to my past. This was a fresh start.

There was a period of readjustment to my new surroundings. Living on my own had given me a real feeling of independence and I had liked the control I had been able to exert on my immediate environment, without the noise or unpredictability of other people to cope with. It was difficult at first to get used to the sounds of my siblings running up and down the stairs or arguing with each other. My mother told each of them to try to respect my need for quiet, and for the most part they did.

My experiences abroad had undoubtedly changed me. For one thing, I had learned a great deal about myself. I could see more clearly than ever before how my 'differentness' affected my day-to-day life, especially my interactions with other people. I had eventually come to understand that friendship was a delicate, gradual process that mustn't be rushed or seized upon but allowed and encouraged to take its course over time. I pictured it as a butterfly, simultaneously beautiful and fragile, that once afloat belonged to the air and any attempt to grab at it would only destroy it. I recalled how in the past at school I had lost potential friendships because, lacking social instinct, I had tried too hard and made completely the wrong impression.

Lithuania had also allowed me to step back from myself and come to terms with my 'differentness' by illustrating the fact that it needn't be a negative thing. As a foreigner I had been able to teach English to my Lithuanian students and tell them all about life in Britain. Not being the same as everyone else had been an advantage to me in Kaunas, and an opportunity to help others.

I also now had a database of widely varied experiences that I could reference in all manner of future

situations. It gave me a greater confidence in my ability
to cope with whatever life might bring to me. The
future wasn't something for me to be afraid of anymore. In my tiny new bedroom at home I felt freer than
ever before.

As a returned volunteer, I was eligible for an end of
service grant for which I had to write about my experience in Lithuania and the things I had learned
whilst there. I sent all the forms back and waited. In
the meantime, I found work as a tutor helping local
children with their reading, writing and arithmetic.
Several months after first applying, I finally received
the grant at the start of 2000. It was just enough money
for a computer; a dream realised for me and the first
my family had ever owned. Once arrived and un-
wrapped, it took some time for me, with the help of
my brothers and father, to piece it all together and get it
working. For the first time I was able to access the
World Wide Web, and was delighted by the sheer
wealth of information now available to me at the click
of a mouse: online encyclopaedias, dictionaries, lists of
trivia, word and number puzzles – they were all there.
So too were message boards and chat rooms.

There is something exciting and reassuring for
individuals on the autistic spectrum about commun-
icating with other people over the Internet. For one
thing, talking in chat rooms or by email does not
require you to know how to initiate a conversation
or when to smile or the numerous intricacies of body

language, as in other social situations. There is no eye contact and it is possible to understand the other person's every word because everything is written down. The use of 'emoticons', such as ☺ and ☹, in chat room conversations also makes it easier to know how the other person is feeling, because he or she tells you in a simple, visual method.

I first met my partner, Neil online in the autumn of 2000. He writes software programmes for a living so uses computers on a daily basis. Like me, Neil is very shy and found the Internet helped him to meet new people and make friends. Almost immediately we began to exchange emails every day, writing about everything from the names of our favourite songs to our hopes and dreams for the future. There was plenty that we had in common and it was not long before he suggested we swap photos and phone numbers. Neil was beautiful: tall with thick, dark hair and shining blue eyes and when I spoke to him over the phone he was always extremely patient, polite and more than happy to do most of the talking. He was nearly the same age as me, twenty-four, and lived and worked in Kent, not far from my home in London. The more I learned about him, the more I remember thinking to myself: I have met my soul mate.

Falling in love is like nothing else; there isn't a right or a wrong way to fall in love with another person, no mathematical equation for love and the perfect relationship. Emotions that I had not experienced in the years since my teenage crush I now felt suddenly and strongly, for long and lingering moments, so profoundly that they hurt. I could not stop thinking about Neil, no matter what I did, and found it difficult even to eat or sleep properly as a result. When he asked me, in an email at the start of 2001, whether we could meet, I hesitated nonetheless. What if the meeting went badly? What if I were to do or say the wrong thing? Was I even someone who could be loved? I did not know.

Before I could answer Neil, I decided I needed to tell my parents about him, which meant I needed to confront them with the truth about myself. The house was quiet that afternoon; my brothers and sisters were all playing outside or upstairs in their rooms, while my mother and father were in the living room watching the television. I had rehearsed what I wanted to say many times over in my head, but entering the room I still felt a pang of sickness because I had no idea what their reaction would be and I do not like situations where anything could happen because they make me feel dizzy and nauseous. Wanting their full attention, I walked over to the television set and switched it off. My father started to complain, but my mother simply looked up and waited for me to speak. Opening my lips, I heard my voice – quiet and cracking – tell them that I was gay and that I had met someone who I liked very much. There was a brief silence when both said nothing but just looked at me. Then my mother told me that it was not a problem and that she wanted me to be happy. My father's reaction was positive too, telling me that he hoped I would find someone I would love and who could love me in return. I hoped so too.

The following week I agreed to meet Neil. It was a cold January morning as I waited for him outside the house, wrapped in a thick coat and wearing a hat and gloves. Just before ten o'clock he pulled up in his car and got out. His first words to me as we shook hands were: 'Your photo doesn't do you justice'. I smiled, though I did not understand the phrase. Neil suggested he drive me down to his home in Kent for the day, so I sat in the passenger seat and we set off. It was a peculiar journey. After a few minutes talking, he lapsed into silence and I did not know how to restart the conversation so I just sat there. I was feeling very nervous and thought to myself: 'He must not like me'. We had driven for over an hour when we reached Neil's home in Ashford, a market town in the centre of Kent. Just then, he leaned behind his seat and lifted out a beautiful bouquet of flowers and gave them to me. So he did like me after all.

Neil's house was part of a modern development, surrounded by other identical-looking houses and a small nearby park with a pond and swings and round-about. Inside, there was striped wallpaper, red carpet and a black-and-white cat called Jay. I kneeled down and stroked her head and she started to purr. Neil took me into the living room and we sat at opposite ends of the sofa and talked. After a while he asked whether I wanted to listen to some music. Gradually, unconsciously, we found ourselves sitting closer and closer together on the sofa, until Neil was holding me in his arms as I rested my head on his shoulder and closed my eyes, listening to the songs. Soon afterwards we kissed. We decided there and then that we were meant to be together. It was the start of something big.

Neil did not find it difficult to accept me for who I was. He too had been bullied at school and knew what it was like to be different from your peers. Being a homebody himself he didn't mind that I preferred the quiet and security of home to the commotion of pubs and clubs. Most important of all, he – like me – had reached a crossroads in his life and wasn't sure about the way forward. Through our chance meeting online we had both of us discovered, to our mutual surprise and joy, that thing that had been missing from both our lives: romantic love.

In the following weeks we continued to email each other daily and to talk regularly on the phone. Whenever he could, Neil would drive up to see me. Six months after we first met, after long discussions together, I made the decision to move to Kent to be with Neil. I walked into the kitchen one day and told my mother matter-of-factly: 'I'm moving out.' My parents were glad for me, but they were also concerned: How would I cope in a relationship with all of the ups and downs and responsibilities that come with it? What mattered at that time were the things that

I knew to be absolutely true: that Neil was a very special person, that I had not ever felt about another person quite how I felt about him, that we loved each other very much and wanted to be together.

The first months after the move were not always easy. Living off a single salary meant that we had to be very careful with our spending. It would be more than two and a half years before we had our first holiday together. During the day, while Neil worked at his office in nearby Ramsgate, I did the chores and cooked in the evenings. I also wrote to all the libraries in the area asking if they had any vacancies, as I very much wanted to work and contribute as much as possible to the costs of running our home. One morning, I received a letter in the post telling me that I had been selected for an interview at a library office where new books were located, ordered and organised for display. On the day of the interview, Neil lent me one of his ties, put it on for me and gave me written instructions for the bus ride to the address given in the letter. Though I got lost walking around various buildings looking for the right one, I eventually made it to the interview with the help of a member of staff who walked me to the correct door.

There was a panel of three interviewers. As one of them started to speak I noticed that she had an accent and asked her about it. When she said that she was originally from Finland, a country I had read a lot about in the library as a child, I began talking non-stop about the things I knew about her native country and even spoke a little Finnish with her. The interview did not last long (which I took as a good sign) and I was excited as I walked out afterwards; after all, I had remembered to maintain eye contact, dressed smartly and been friendly throughout. I was devastated when a few days later I received a phone call telling me that I had not been chosen for the position. Dozens of detailed, handwritten applications for other positions in libraries, schools and colleges over the following months were all rejected or went unanswered.

Unfortunately, my experience is commonplace. Research in 2001 by the UK's National Autistic Society indicated that only 12% of those with high-functioning autism or Asperger's syndrome had full-time jobs. In contrast, 49% of people with other disabilities and 81% of people who are not disabled were in employment in 2003, according to the UK's Office for National Statistics. There are several important reasons for this disparity. Individuals with an autistic spectrum disorder often have problems finding out about job opportunities or understanding the confusing jargon that frequently appears in job adverts. Interviews for selection require communication and social interaction skills, which are particular areas of difficulty for someone with autism. The National Autistic Society's Employment Information sheet suggests a work trial instead of a formal interview as a fairer alternative. Questions in an interview can also be hard to follow and answer adequately. Several of the questions I was asked in my interview related to hypothetical situations, which I found difficult to imagine and could only reply to briefly. It would be a lot better if questions instead focused on actual past experience to demonstrate what the person already knows.

People on the autistic spectrum can bring many benefits to a job in a company or organisation: reliability, honesty, a high level of accuracy, considerable attention to detail and a good knowledge of various facts and figures. Firms who employ individuals with autism/Asperger's help to raise awareness of diversity among their staff, while managers with autistic employees often find that they learn to communicate with their whole team more effectively.

The lack of money was not an insurmountable problem for us. In particular, Neil always made every effort to be encouraging and supportive towards me, reassuring me when I felt frustrated or sad and gently pushing me to look constructively ahead to the future. At Christmas 2001, I met Neil's parents and family for the first time. I felt very nervous, but Neil kept telling me that I had nothing to worry about. We drove to his parents' home, not far from our own, and were greeted at the door by his mother, who showed me around and introduced me to the other family members: Neil's father, brother, sister-in-law and young niece. Everyone was smiling and I felt calm and happy. There was a very large and tasty meal, followed by an exchange of cards and presents. The following day, Neil drove us up to London to visit my family and it was Neil's turn to be introduced to my parents and brothers and sisters, who were all excited to meet him. The support from both our families meant a great deal to both Neil and myself.

The following summer we moved to a small, quiet coastal town called Herne Bay, close to the historical city of Canterbury. Moving house is always a very stressful period in a person's life and it was no different for me. The first weeks after we arrived at our new house were very disruptive, with furniture and paint and boxes spread all around the house and little opportunity to stop and relax. When Neil was busy with something practical, I helped by making food and tea and fetching things from around the house for him. This also helped me to forget about any anxiety I was experiencing by making me focus on the things that I could do, rather than worry about the things that I could not. It was exciting to watch the transformation, as the house became a home.

I feel very fortunate to have the small band of close friends that I do. With email, I am able to stay in regular or irregular contact with distant friends, such as Rehan and Birutė. More recent friendships have all been accidental, in a way, like a wonderful surprise gift. For example, one of my closest friends today (his name is Ian) was a childhood neighbour of Neil's. One day, shortly after the move to Herne Bay, we received a postcard from him forwarded from Neil's parents. Ian and Neil had not seen each other for fifteen years, yet when we invited him over one evening it was as if they had never been apart. We soon learned that I had several things in common with Ian, such as a love of books and of history, and we have been close friends ever since.

It is great when I discover that I can put some of my abilities to good use in helping my friends. When Ian recently married a Romanian woman, he asked me if I would help him approach the matter of learning some of his new wife's mother tongue. In return, Ian takes me to play golf with him at weekends. I am not a very good player, though my putting is pretty good. Sometimes Ian scratches his head when he sees me walking backwards on a putting green from my ball to the hole. What I'm doing is feeling the way that the ground moves through my feet; then I have a better idea of how the ball will move once I strike it with my putter. It works for me.

Our friends are aware of my Asperger's and try, whenever possible, to ensure that I am comfortable in any social situation with them. Often they will arrange get-togethers that they know I will enjoy as much as they do. Every year, Neil and another friend called Ian organise a treasure hunt in association with their Mini car club and invite me to join in. Each team is given a list of clues and questions that are solved by driving to different locations marked on a map and finding the answers. For example, one clue might read: 'Young equine's accommodation', the answer to which is revealed by driving past a pub with the name 'Colt's House'. As Ian drives, Neil gives directions while I help to find and figure out the answers to the questions. It feels good to do something that everyone can enjoy for different reasons.

Whenever we visit our friends we usually play a game after supper, such as cards or Trivial Pursuit. Neil says it is good manners to let your hosts win, but I don't understand that because if you know the answer to a question, then why not go for it?

I love doing quizzes and enjoy watching programmes such as *Who Wants To Be A Millionaire?* on the television. I usually know the answer to most of the questions, but I do have my weak points, such as pop music and fiction. My favourite questions are those involving dates ('What year did the World Snooker Championship first take place at the Crucible Theatre?' Answer: '1977') or chronology ('Put these four historical events in the order in which they occurred').

Not long after the move to Herne Bay, Neil and I decided to work together on an idea that I had had to create an educational website with online courses for language learners. Neil, with his job in computers, would be responsible for all the technical details, while I would write the site's content and the courses. After some thought, I chose the name 'Optimnem' for the site, from 'Mnemosyne', the inventor of words and language in Greek mythology. The students receive each lesson by email and these come with audio clips recorded by native speakers, lots of written examples of the language, and exercises to help practise and revise at each step of the course. In creating each of the courses, I was able to draw on the experience that I had had as a teacher in Lithuania and as a tutor to help me focus on the parts of language learning that people often find most difficult. I also wanted to write courses that reflected my own personal experiences as a learner on the autistic spectrum. For these reasons, each course is broken down into easily digested chunks of information. The lessons avoid jargon such as 'nominative' and 'genitive' or 'verb conjugation' and instead try to explain how words change, depending for example on their position in a sentence, in simple and clear language. Using lots of written examples also means students can see the language at work in many different situations and it is easier to remember new vocabulary when it is presented visually and in context. The website was launched in September 2002 and proved a success, with thousands of students of all ages and from all over the world using it, and millions of 'hits' (page views). Optimnem is now in its fourth year and is an approved member of the UK's National Grid for Learning, a government-funded portal that provides 'a gateway to educationally valuable content on the Internet'.

The success of the website meant that I was working and earning money, something that I felt proud and excited about. There was also the benefit of working from home, which is definitely an advantage for me because of the anxiety I can feel when I am in an environment that I cannot control and do not feel comfortable in. I'm happy to be self-employed, though of course it is not an easy choice and it can be much harder to achieve financial independence this way.

Neil too now works from home, only needing to commute to and from his office in Ramsgate once a week. On an average weekday, I sit with my computer at the kitchen table at the back of the house with a beautiful view over the garden, while Neil works in the office (a converted bedroom) upstairs. If I need advice over something relating to the website, it is only a short walk up the stairs to ask him. Seeing so much of each other is a good thing for us, though I know it would not work for every relationship. For lunch, we sit together and talk over our sandwiches or soup, which I prepare. Neil is happy to occasionally share in my obsessive daily routines: drinking tea with me at the same times each day for example. After work, we make supper in the kitchen together, which gives us both a chance to relax and think about other things.

I have always loved animals, from my childhood fascination with ladybirds to avidly watching wildlife programmes on television. I think one reason is that animals are often more patient and accepting than many people. After I first moved in with Neil, I spent a lot of time with his cat, Jay. She was then a little less than two years old and very aloof, preferring to spend all her time out wandering around the neighbourhood gardens and growling whenever Neil tried to pat or hold her. At that time, Neil was working at his office and was away from the house for ten or more hours each day. Before my arrival, Jay had therefore spent her first and formative years alone for much of the time. It must have been a surprise, then – and a shock – for her to suddenly find that she now had company throughout the day. At first I kept my distance, knowing that she was unused to having someone around regularly. Instead, I waited for her natural curiosity to start to work and indeed it wasn't long before she would walk up to me as I was sitting in the living room, and sniff at my feet, and hands if I lowered them for her to rub with her nose. Over time, Jay started to spend more and more time indoors. Whenever she came in, I would kneel down until my face was level with hers and slowly extend my hand around her head and stroke her in the same way that I had watched her stroke the fur on her back with her tongue. Then she would purr and open and close her eyes sleepily and I knew that I had won her affection.

Jay was a smart and sensitive cat. Sometimes I lay down on the floor for her to sit on my chest or tummy and snooze. Just before she sat down, she would pummel me gently with her paws. This is a common behaviour in cats, known as 'treading' or 'padding', and is thought to indicate contentment. The reasons for it are not clear; though the action mimics the way a kitten uses its paws to stimulate the flow of milk from its mother's teat. Once Jay was sitting on me, I would close my eyes and slow down my breathing so that she thought I was dozing too. She would then feel reassured, because she knew that I would not be making any sudden movements, and relax and stay close to me. Often I wore one of my thick, coarse sweaters, even in warm weather, because I knew that Jay preferred their texture to smooth t-shirts or other clothes.

For all her affection, at various times Jay could still be remote and indifferent towards us and especially towards Neil, something that I knew upset him very much. I suggested to him that what she needed was a companion, another cat to interact with. I hoped that she would learn social skills in the process and become more approachable. We read the adverts in the local newspaper and saw one from someone with a cat that had recently borne a litter of kittens. We telephoned and made an appointment to go and view them. When we arrived at the house the next day we were told that most of them had been sold already and only a couple remained. I pointed to one, a tiny, shy black kitten, and was told that nobody had shown any interest in her because she was black all over. We agreed straight away to take her home with us and gave her the name

Moomin. At first, unsurprisingly, Jay was not sure of her new sister and hissed and growled at her at every opportunity. Over time, however, she stopped and began to at least tolerate her presence. What became even more heartening, though, was the gradual but definite change in her overall behaviour: she became much more affectionate, willing to be picked up and held, and much happier, with long, loud periods of purring and bouts of playfulness with Moomin and with us. She would make a wonderful 'brrrp' sound whenever she saw us, to which I would respond by crouching down and rubbing my face against the fur on hers.

In the summer of 2004, we celebrated Jay's fifth birthday, giving her extra food and toys to play with. However, her appetite seemed smaller and her energy lower than usual, which we thought might be due to the very hot weather. She often sat or slept under something: a bed, or a table, or the towel rack in the bathroom. I understood this behaviour very well, because as a child I too had climbed under my bed or a table to help me feel calm and secure. But then Jay was doing it more and more, becoming withdrawn from us in the process. Then came the sickness. She would vomit repeatedly but only liquid would come out. At first it was a nuisance, but then as it went on we began to worry. By now she was also losing weight and walking more slowly around the house. Neil took her to the vet and she was kept in for tests and observation. We soon heard that she had a kidney infection, rare in a cat so young, and that she would need several days of treatment on site. We phoned every day for an update on her condition and were told that she was stable. Then, a week after we took her in, we received a call telling us that Jay was not responding to the treatment and that it might be a good idea for us both to come in and see her.

We drove over immediately. A woman at reception walked us through a narrow corridor to a quiet, grey room at the back of the building, then said she would leave us alone for a few minutes. Even at that moment, I do not think the seriousness of the situation had really occurred to me. As Neil and I stood there in the middle of the room in mutual silence, I saw her. Jay was lying still on a white mattress surrounded by plastic tubes, growling weakly and repeatedly. Hesitantly, I reached out my hand and stroked her; her fur felt greasy and underneath she was thin and bony. Suddenly, like a wave hitting a rock from out of sight, I felt an emotion inside too big for me to contain and my face was wet and I knew that I was crying. Neil walked over and stared at her, then he too began to weep softly. A nurse came in and told us that they were doing everything they could, but that Jay's condition was rare and very serious. We drove home and cried again on each other's shoulders. The next day Neil received a call telling him that Jay had passed away. There were many more tears in the days that followed, as well as the abiding shock over losing a companion so deeply loved so suddenly and unexpectedly. She was cremated and we buried her ashes in the garden with a stone monument dedicated to her memory. It reads: 'Jay, 1999–2004. Always in our hearts.'

No relationship is without its difficulties and this is certainly true when one or both of the persons involved has an autistic spectrum disorder. Even so, I believe what is truly essential to the success of any relationship is not so much compatibility, but love. When you love someone, virtually anything is possible.

There are seemingly trivial situations at home, such as dropping a spoon while doing the washing up, when I will have a meltdown and need time to stop and calm down before I can continue. Even a small, unexpected loss of control can feel overwhelming to me, particularly when it interferes with the rhythm of one of my routines. Neil has learned not to intervene but to let it pass, which does not normally take very long, and his patience helps a lot. With his support and understanding, such meltdowns have become less frequent over time.

Other situations can cause me high levels of anxiety, if for example a friend or neighbour spontaneously decides to come over to see us. Although I am happy to see him or her, I can feel myself go tense and become flustered, because it means I have to change the schedule I had already mapped out in my head for that day, and having to alter my plans is unsettling for me. Again Neil reassures me and helps me to stay calm.

Social situations can be a big problem for me. If we eat in a restaurant, I prefer to sit at a table in the corner or against a wall so other diners do not surround me. During one visit to a local restaurant, we were talking and eating happily when suddenly I smelled cigarette smoke. I could not see where it was coming from, had not anticipated it, and became very anxious. Neil notices when this happens because he has seen it many times before: I drop my eye contact and become monosyllabic. There was nothing to do but to eat up and leave as soon as possible. I am fortunate that we both enjoy spending a lot of time together at home and do not need to go out very much. When we do, it is usually to a cinema or a quiet restaurant.

Conversations can be problematic between us because of the auditory processing difficulties I sometimes experience. Neil will say something to me, to which I will nod or say 'yes' or 'okay', but then later I will realise that I have not understood what he said. It can be very frustrating for him to spend time explaining or recounting something important to me, only to find afterwards that I have not taken it in. The problem is that I do not realise that I am not hearing what he is saying; I very often hear fragments of each sentence, which my brain automatically pulls together to try to make sense of. By missing key words, however, I quite often do not get the real content of what is being said.

Nodding and saying things like 'okay' when someone is speaking to me has evolved over time as my way of allowing communication between me and someone else to flow normally, without the other person needing to stop and repeat continuously. Though the tactic works for me most of the time, I now realise that it is not appropriate within a relationship. Instead, Neil and I have learned to persevere when we talk together: I give my fullest attention to him while he is speaking to me and signal if there is a word or words that need to be repeated. That way, we can both be sure that each of us understands the other fully.

As a teenager, I hated having to shave. The blades would rub against my face and cut me as I struggled to hold the razor securely with one hand while holding my head still with the other. It would often take longer than an hour at a time to shave, after which my skin would feel hot and itchy. It was so uncomfortable that I shaved as infrequently as possible, sometimes going for months until my beard – as the stubble became – pulled on the skin and irritated it so much that I had to shave it off. In the end, I shaved around twice a month, often annoying my brothers and sisters because I would take so long in the bathroom. Nowadays, Neil shaves me every week with an electric razor that trims the stubble and is quick and not painful to me.

Being extra sensitive to certain physical sensations affects the ways in which Neil and I express affection and intimacy towards each other. For example, I find light touching – such as a finger stroking my arm – uncomfortable and I had to explain this to Neil because of the way I would squirm when all he was trying to do was demonstrate his love for me. Fortunately, it is no problem for me to hold hands or to have Neil put his arm lightly around me.

I have learned a huge amount from Neil in the years that we have been together and from the experience of loving him and sharing our lives with one another. Love has definitely changed me by making me more open to others and more aware of the world around me. It has also made me more confident in myself and in my ability to grow and make new progress day by day. Neil is a part of my world, part of what makes me 'me', and I could not for one moment imagine my life without him.

9

The Gift of Tongues

Languages had always been a source of fascination to me and having now settled into my new home and established the website I could really begin to spend more time working on them. The first language I studied after Lithuanian was Spanish. My interest in it was piqued by a conversation that I had with Neil's mother, in which she talked of holidays the family had taken in various parts of Spain and mentioned that she had been learning the language over many years. I asked if she had any books that I could borrow and she found an old 'Teach Yourself' title for me to take away and read. The following week we visited Neil's parents again and I returned the book to his mother. When I began conversing with her comfortably in Spanish she couldn't believe it.

I used a similar method to learn Romanian, which I began after my friend Ian asked me for advice on learning the language to help him communicate with his wife, Ana. I supplemented my reading with an online Romanian language edition of the Saint-Exupéry classic, *Micul Print* (*The Little Prince*).

My latest language-learning project is Welsh, a beautiful and distinctive language that I first heard and saw during a holiday with Neil to the small North Wales town of Blaenau Ffestiniog, in the mountains of Snowdonia. Many of the people in this area speak Welsh as their first language (overall one in five people in Wales speak Welsh) and it was the only language that I heard spoken in many of the places that we visited.

Welsh has a number of features that are unique among all the languages I have studied. Words beginning with certain consonants sometimes change their first letters, depending on how they are used in a sentence. For example, the word *ceg* ('mouth') changes to *dy geg* ('your mouth'), *fy ngheg* ('my mouth') and *ei cheg* ('her mouth'). The word order in Welsh is also unusual, with the verb coming first in a sentence: *Aeth Neil i Aberystwyth* ('Neil went to Aberystwyth', literally 'went Neil to Aberystwyth'). I've found the hardest part of learning Welsh is the pronunciation of certain sounds, such as 'll', which is rather like putting your tongue in position to say the letter 'l' and then trying to say the letter 's'.

An invaluable resource for my Welsh study has been the Welsh language television channel S4C which I'm able to watch through my satellite receiver. Programmes are varied and interesting, from the soap opera *Pobol y Cwm* (*People of the Valley*) to the *newyddion* (news). It has proven an excellent way for me to improve my comprehension and pronunciation skills.

The relationship I have with a language is quite an aesthetic one, with certain words and combinations of words being particularly beautiful and stimulating to me. Sometimes I will read a sentence in a book over and over again, because of the way the words make me feel inside. Nouns are my favourite type of words, because they are the easiest for me to visualise.

When I'm learning a language there are a number of things that I consider essential materials to begin with. The first is a good size dictionary. I also need a variety of texts in the language, such as children's books, stories and newspaper articles, because I prefer to learn words within whole sentences to help give me a feeling for how the language works. I have an excellent visual memory and when I read a word or phrase or sentence written down, I close my eyes, see it in my head and can remember it perfectly. My memory is much poorer if I can only hear a word or phrase and not see it. Conversing with native speakers helps to improve accent, pronunciation and comprehension. I do not mind making mistakes but try very hard not to repeat them once they have been pointed out to me.

Each language can act as a stepping-stone to another. The more languages a person knows, the easier it becomes to learn a new one. This is because languages are somewhat like people: they belong to 'families' of related languages, which share certain similarities. Languages also influence and borrow from each other. Even before I began to study Romanian, I could understand perfectly the sentence: *Unde este un creion galben?* ('Where is a yellow pencil?'), because of the similarities to Spanish: *dónde está* ('where is?'), French: *un crayon* ('a pencil') and German: *gelb* ('yellow').

There are also relationships between words inside each language which are unique to it. I am able to see these connections easily. For example, Icelandic has *borð* ('table') and *borða* ('to eat'), French has *jour* ('day') and *journal* ('newspaper') and German has *Hand* ('hand') and *Handel* (a 'trade' or 'craft').

Learning compound words can help to enrich vocabulary and provide useful examples of a language's grammar. The German word for vocabulary, as an example, is *Wortschatz*, combining the words *Wort* ('word') and *Schatz* ('treasure'). In Finnish, compounds can be formed that are equivalent to many separate words in other languages. For example, in the sentence: *Hän oli talossanikin* ('He was in my house too') the last word *talossanikin* is composed of four separate parts: *talo* ('house') + -ssa ('in') + -*ni* ('my') and -*kin* ('too').

I find some aspects of language much more difficult than others. Abstract words are much harder for me to understand and I have a picture in my head for each that helps me to make sense of the meaning. For example, the word 'complexity' makes me think of a braid or plait of hair – the many different strands woven together into a complete whole. When I read or hear that something is complex I imagine it as having lots of different parts that need tying together to arrive at an answer. Similarly, the word 'triumph' creates a picture in my mind of a large, golden trophy, such as the ones won in big sporting events. If I hear about a politician's 'election triumph' I imagine the politician holding a trophy over his head, like the winning team captain at an FA cup final. For the word 'fragile' I think of glass; I picture a 'fragile peace' as a glass dove. The image I see helps me to understand that the peace might be shattered at any moment.

Certain sentence structures can be particularly hard for me to analyse, such as: 'He is not inexperienced in such things', where the two negatives ('not' and 'in-') cancel each other out. It is much better if people just say: 'He is experienced in such things'. Another example is when a sentence begins: 'Don't you . . .?' as in, 'Don't you think we should go now?' or 'Don't you want ice cream?'. Then I become very confused and my head starts to hurt because the questioner is not being clear whether he means: 'Do you want an ice cream?' or 'Is it correct that you don't want an ice cream?' and it's possible to answer both questions with a 'yes', but I don't like it when the same word can mean two completely different things.

As a child, I found idiomatic language particularly confusing. Describing someone as 'under the weather' was very strange to me because, I thought, isn't everyone under the weather? Another common saying that puzzled me was when my parents might excuse one of my brother's grumpy behaviour by saying: 'He must have got out of the wrong side of bed this morning.' 'Why didn't he get out of the right side of the bed?' I asked.

In recent years, scientists have become more and more interested in studying the kind of synaesthetic experiences in language that I have, in order to find out more about the phenomenon and its origins. Professor Vilayanur Ramachandran of California's Center for Brain Studies in San Diego, has researched synaesthesia for more than a decade and believes there may be a link between the neurological basis for synaesthetic experiences and the linguistic creativity of poets and writers. According to one study, the condition is seven times as common in creative people as in the general population.

In particular, Professor Ramachandran points to the

facility with which creative writers think up and use metaphors – a form of language where a comparison is made between two seemingly unrelated things – and compares this to the linking of seemingly unrelated entities such as colours and words, or shapes and numbers in synaesthesia.

Some scientists believe that high-level concepts (including numbers and language) are anchored in specific regions of the brain and that synaesthesia might be caused by excess communication between these different regions. Such 'crossed wiring' could lead to both synaesthesia and to a propensity toward the making of links between seemingly unrelated ideas.

William Shakespeare, for example, was a frequent user of metaphors; many of which are synaesthetic, involving a link to the senses. For example, in *Hamlet*, Shakespeare has the character Francisco say that it is 'bitter cold' – combining the sensation of coldness with the taste of bitterness. In another play, *The Tempest*, Shakespeare goes beyond metaphors involving only the senses and links concrete experiences with more abstract ideas. His expression: 'This music crept by me upon the waters,' connects the abstract 'music' with a creeping action. The reader is able to imagine music – something normally very difficult to create a mental picture of – as a moving animal.

But it isn't only very creative people who make these connections – everyone does. We all rely on synaesthesia to a greater or lesser degree. In their book

Metaphors We Live By, language scientist George Lakoff and philosopher Mark Johnson argue that metaphors are not arbitrary constructions but follow particular patterns, which in turn structure thought. They give as examples expressions that indicate the links: 'happy' = 'up' and 'sad' = 'down': *I'm feeling up, my spirits rose; I'm feeling down, he's really low.* Or 'more' = 'up' and 'less' = 'down': *My income rose last year; the number of errors is very low.* Lakoff and Johnson suggest that many of these patterns emerge from our everyday, physical experiences; for example, the link 'sad' = 'down' may be related to the way that posture droops when a person is feeling sad. Similarly, the link 'more' = 'up' may come from the fact that when you add an object or substance to a container or pile, the level goes up.

Other language scientists have noted that some of the structural features of many words not normally associated with any function, such as initial phoneme groups, have a noticeable affect on the reader/listener. For example for 'sl-' there is: 'slack', 'slouch', 'sludge', 'slime', 'slosh', 'sloppy', 'slug', 'slut', 'slang', 'sly', 'slow', 'sloth', 'sleepy', 'slipshod', 'slovenly', 'slum', 'slobber', 'slur', 'slog' . . . where all these words have negative connotations and some are particularly pejorative.

The idea that certain types of sounds 'fit' particular objects better than others goes back to the time of the Ancient Greeks. An obvious illustration of this is onomatopoeia, a type of word that sounds like the thing it is describing ('fizz', 'whack', 'bang' etc.). In a test carried out by researchers in the 1960s, artificial words were constructed using particular letters and combinations of letters thought to link to positive or negative feelings. After hearing the invented words, the subjects were asked to match English words for pleasant or unpleasant emotions with one or other of two invented words. The appropriate matches were made significantly more often than would be expected by chance.

This type of latent language synaesthesia in virtually everyone can also be seen in an experiment originally carried out in the 1920s, which investigated a possible link between visual patterns and the sound-structures of words. The researcher, Wolfgang Köhler, a German-American psychologist, used two arbitrary visual shapes, one smooth and rounded and the other sharp and angular, and invented two words for them: 'takete' and 'maluma'. Subjects were asked to say which of the shapes was the 'takete' and which the 'maluma'. The overwhelming majority assigned 'maluma' to the rounded shape and 'takete' to the angular one. Recently, Professor Ramachandran's team has replicated the results of this test using the invented words 'bouba' and 'kiki'. 95% of those asked thought the rounded shape was a 'bouba' and the pointed shape a 'kiki'. Ramachandran suggests the reason is that the sharp changes in the visual direction

of the lines in the 'kiki' figure mimics the sharp pho-
nemic inflections of the word's sound, as well as the
sharp inflection of the tongue on the palate.

Professor Ramachandran believes this synaesthetic
connection between our hearing and seeing senses
was an important first step towards the creation of
words in early humans. According to this theory, our
ancestors would have begun to talk by using sounds
that evoked the object they wanted to describe. He also
points out that lip and tongue movements may be
synaesthetically linked to objects and events they refer
to. For example, words referring to something small
often involve making a synaesthetic small 'i' sound with
the lips and a narrowing of the vocal tracts: 'little',
'teeny', 'petite', whereas the opposite is true of words
denoting something large or enormous. If the theory is
right then language emerged from the vast array of
synaesthetic connections in the human brain.

An interesting question that language researchers are
beginning to explore is whether or not my ability with

languages extends to other forms of language, such as sign language. In 2005 I participated in an experiment carried out by Gary Morgan of the Department of Language and Communication Science at City University in London. Dr Morgan is a researcher in British Sign Language (BSL), the first or preferred language of around 70,000 deaf or hearing-impaired people in the UK. Many thousands of hearing people also use BSL, which is a visual/spatial language that uses the hands, body, face and head to convey meaning. The test was designed to see whether I could learn signed words as quickly and easily as written or spoken ones. A signer sat opposite me at a table and produced a total of sixty-eight different signs. After each I was shown a page with four illustrations and asked to indicate the one that I thought best described the sign I had just been shown. The signed words varied in meaning from the relatively simple 'hat' to more difficult signs for concepts such as 'restaurant' and 'agriculture'. I was able to correctly identify two-thirds of the signs from the possible choices presented to me and it was concluded that I showed 'very good sign aptitude'. The researchers now plan to teach me British Sign Language using one-to-one tuition with a signer to compare my acquisition of the language with that of the others I know.

Esperanto is another very different kind of language. I first read the word 'Esperanto' many years ago in a library book, but it was only following the purchase of my first computer that I discovered any more about it. What drew me most of all to the language was the fact that its vocabulary is a blend of various languages, mostly European, while its grammar is consistent and logical. I very quickly *esperantiĝis* (became a speaker of Esperanto) from reading various online texts in the language and from writing to other Esperanto speakers from all over the world.

The Esperanto language (the word means 'one who hopes') was the creation of Dr Ludovic Lazarus Zamenhof, an eye doctor from Bialystok in what is now Poland. He first published his language in 1887 and the first world congress of Esperanto speakers was held in France in 1905. Zamenhof's goal was to create an easy-to-learn universal second language to help foster international understanding. Today, there are estimated to be somewhere between 100,000 and 1,000,000 Esperanto speakers worldwide.

Esperanto's grammar has several interesting features. The first is that the different parts of speech are marked by their own suffixes: all nouns end in -o, all adjectives in -a, adverbs in -e, infinitives in -i. For example: the word *rapido* would translate as 'speed', *rapida* as 'quick', *rapide* as 'quickly' and *rapidi* as 'to hurry'.

Verbs do not change for the subject, as in most natural languages: *mi estas* ('I am'), *vi estas* ('you are'), *li estas* ('he is'), *ŝi estas* ('she is'), *ni estas* ('we are'), *ili estas* ('they are'). Past tense verbs always end in -is (*mi estis* – 'I was'), future tense in -os (*vi estos* – 'you will be').

Many of Esperanto's words are formed using affixes – the ending '-ejo', for example, signifies 'place', as in the words: *lernejo* ('school'), *infanejo* ('nursery') and *trinkejo* ('bar'). Another commonly used suffix is '-ilo', meaning 'tool or instrument', and is found in words such as: *hakilo* ('axe'), *flugilo* ('wing') and *serĉilo* ('search engine').

Perhaps the most famous feature of Esperanto's word-building grammar is its use of the prefix 'mal-' to indicate the opposite of something. This feature is used extensively throughout the language: *bona* ('good') – *malbona* ('evil'), *riĉa* ('rich') – *malriĉa* ('poor'), *granda* ('big') – *malgranda* ('small'), *dekstra* ('right') – *maldekstra* ('left'), *fermi* ('to close') – *malfermi* ('to open'), *amiko* ('friend') – *malamiko* ('enemy').

The creation and use of idiomatic speech is generally discouraged in Esperanto, however some examples of 'Esperanto slang' do exist. A new learner of the language might be called a *freŝbakito* from the German *frischgebacken* ('fresh-baked'), where the standard Esperanto word would be a *komencanto* ('beginner'). An example of an Esperanto euphemism is *la necesejo* ('the necessary place') for a bathroom/WC.

Tony Attwood, a clinical psychologist and author of *Asperger's Syndrome: A Guide for Parents and Professionals*, notes that some individuals with Asperger's have the ability to create their own form of language (known as neologisms). He gives as examples a girl's description of her ankle as 'the wrist of my foot' and ice cubes as 'water bones'. Dr Attwood describes this ability as 'one of the endearing and genuinely creative aspects of Asperger's syndrome'. After the birth of my twin sisters I created the word *biplets* to describe them, knowing that a bicycle had two wheels and a tricycle three, and that the name for three babies born at one time was triplets. Another of my childhood neologisms was the word *pramble* meaning to go out for a long walk (a ramble) with a baby in a pram; something my parents did frequently.

For several years as a child I tinkered with the idea of creating my own language, as a way of relieving the loneliness I often felt and to draw on the delight I experienced in words. Sometimes, when I felt a particularly strong emotion or experienced something that I felt was especially beautiful, a new word would spontaneously form in my mind to express it and I had no idea where those words came from. In contrast, I often found the language of my peers jarring and confusing. I was regularly teased for speaking in long, careful and overly formal sentences. When I tried to use one of my own created words in conversation, to express something of what I was feeling or experiencing inside, it was rarely understood. My parents discouraged me from 'talking in a funny way'.

I continued to dream that one day I would speak a

language that was my own, that I would not be teased or reprimanded for using and that would express something of what it felt to be me. After leaving school I found I had the time to begin seriously to pursue such an idea. I wrote words down as they occurred to me and experimented with different methods of pronunciation and sentence building. I called my language 'Mänti' (pronounced '*man*-tee') from the Finnish word *mänty* meaning pine tree. Pines are native to most of the Northern hemisphere and are particularly numerous across parts of Scandinavia and the Baltic region. Many of the words used in Mänti are of Scandinavian and Baltic origin. There is another reason for the choice of name: pine trees often grow together in large numbers and symbolise friendship and community.

Mänti is a work in progress with a developed grammar and a vocabulary of more than a thousand words. It has attracted the interest of several language researchers who believe it may help shed more light on my linguistic abilities.

One of the things I like most about playing with language is the creation of new words and ideas. I try in Mänti to make the words reflect the relationships between different things: *hamma* ('tooth') and *hemme* ('ant' – a biting insect) and *rât* ('wire') and *râtio* ('radio') for example. Some words have multiple, related meanings; the word *puhu* for example can mean 'wind', 'breath' or 'spirit'.

Compound words are common in Mänti: *puhekello*

('telephone', literally 'speak-bell'), *ilmalāv* ('aeroplane', literally 'airship'), *tontöö* ('music', literally 'tone art') and *rātalö* ('parliament', literally 'discussion place') are various examples.

Abstracts are handled in a number of ways in Mänti. One is to create a compound to describe it: 'tardiness' or 'lateness' is translated as *kellokült* (literally 'clock-debt'). Another method is to use 'word pairs', as can be found in Finno-Ugrian languages such as Estonian. For a word such as 'dairy (produce)' the Mänti equivalent is *pîmat kermat* ('milks creams') and for 'footwear' it is *koet saapat* ('shoes boots').

Although Mänti is very different from English, there are quite a lot of words that are recognisable to English speakers: *nekka* ('neck'), *kuppi* ('cup'), *purssi* ('wallet'), *nööt* ('night') and *pêpi* ('baby') are examples.

Mänti exists as a tangible, communicable expression of my inner world. Each word, shining with colour and texture, to me is like a piece of art. When I think or speak in Mänti, I feel as though I am painting in words.

10

A Very Large Slice of Pi

I first learned about the number pi in my maths class at school. Pi – the ratio of a circle's circumference to its diameter – is mathematics' most celebrated number; the name comes from the sixteenth letter of the Greek alphabet (π), the symbol being adopted by the mathematician Euler in 1737. I was immediately fascinated by it and learned as many of its decimal digits as I could find from various library books, hundreds of them in total. Then, in late 2003, I received a phone call from my father who reminded me at the end of the conversation that it had been twenty years since my early childhood seizures. He said that I should be proud of the progress I had made in the time since. I thought about what he said for a long time afterwards and decided that I wanted to do something to show that my childhood experience of epilepsy had not held me back. Later that week I contacted the fundraising department of the National Society for Epilepsy, the largest epilepsy charity organisation in the UK. To help raise funds for the NSE, my plan was to learn as many digits of the number pi as I could in correct sequence, before a public recitation in three months' time, on 14 March – International Pi Day (14 March is 3/14 in US notation) – which is also Einstein's birthday. The charity was excited by the idea and suggested that I attempt to break the European record, so a target of 22,500 digits was set. While I began learning the numbers, the charity's fundraising manager Simon Ekless organised the setting for the recitation, the Ashmolean Building at the Museum of the History of Science in Oxford, where among the various exhibits is one of Albert Einstein's blackboards.

Pi is an irrational number, which means that it cannot be written as a simple fraction of two whole numbers. It is also infinite: the digits to the right of the decimal point go on forever in a never-ending numerical stream, so that it isn't possible for someone to write down the number pi exactly, even if he or she had a piece of paper as big as the universe to write it on. For this reason, calculations must always use approximations of pi, such as $22 \div 7$ or $355 \div 113$. The number appears in all sorts of unexpected places in mathematics besides circles and spheres. For example, it occurs in the distribution of primes and in the probability that a pin dropped on a set of parallel lines will intersect a line. Pi also appears as the average ratio of the actual length and the direct distance between source and mouth in a meandering river.

The earliest values of pi were almost certainly found by measurement. There is good evidence that the ancient Egyptians had $4(8/9)^2 = 3.16$ as a value for pi, while the Babylonians used the approximation $3 + 1/8 = 3.125$. The Greek mathematician Archimedes of Syracuse gave the first theoretical calculation for the value of pi in around 250 BC. He determined the upper and lower range of pi by finding the perimeters of a polygon inscribed within a circle, which is less than the circumference of a circle (Fig.1) and of a polygon circumscribed outside a circle, which is greater than the circumference (Fig.2).

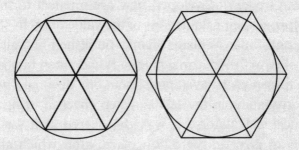

By doubling the number of sides of the hexagon to a dodecagon (twelve sides), then a twenty-four and forty-eight-sided polygon, and finally up to a ninety-

six-sided polygon, Archimedes brought the two perimeters closer and closer in length to the circle's circumference, thereby arriving at his approximation. He
calculated that pi was less than 3 1/7 but greater than 3
10/71. This translates in decimal notation to between
3.1408 and 3.1429 (rounded up to four decimal
places), which is very close to the actual value of
3.1416.

During the Middle Ages, the German mathematician Ludolph van Ceulen spent a large part of his life
calculating the numerical value of pi, using essentially
the same methods as the ones employed by Archimedes some 1800 years before. In 1596, he gave a
value of pi to 20 decimal places in his book *Van den
Circkel* (*On the Circle*), which he later expanded to 35
decimals. After his death, the digits were engraved on
his tombstone.

Later mathematicians, including Isaac Newton and
James Gregory, developed new arithmetical formulas
to improve their calculations of the value of pi. In 1873,
the Englishman William Shanks published his calculation of pi to 707 decimal places. It had taken him more
than fifteen years, averaging about one decimal a week.
Unfortunately, in the 1940s, when checked using me-
chanical calculators, it was discovered that he had
made an error in the 528th place, after which all his
subsequent digits were wrong.

With the advent of modern computers, it became
possible to calculate pi to much greater values than ever

before. The first computer calculation of pi was performed in 1949 on ENIAC (Electronic Numerical Integrator and Computer) – a huge machine that weighed 30 tons and was the size of a small house – calculating to 2,037 decimal places in seventy hours. Since then, rapid improvements in computer technology have helped researchers compute pi to an ever-increasing number of digits. In 2002, computer scientist Yasumasa Kanada and his coworkers at the University of Tokyo Information Technology Centre computed pi to more than one trillion decimal places.

Over the years, many pi enthusiasts have attempted to memorise some of the number's infinite string of digits. The most common method uses sentences and even whole poems composed of carefully chosen words, with the number of letters in each representing successive digits of pi. Perhaps the most famous example is the following, attributed to the British mathematician Sir James Jeans:

How I want a drink, alcoholic of course, after the heavy lectures involving quantum mechanics!

Where the word 'How' = 3 (having three letters) and 'I' 1 and 'want' 4, the complete sentence translating to 3.14159265358979, which is pi to 14 decimal places.

Another (first published in 1905) gives pi to 30 decimal places:

Sir, I send a rhyme excelling
In sacred truth and rigid spelling
Numerical sprites elucidate
For me the lexicon's dull weight
If Nature gain
Not you complain,
Tho' Dr Johnson fulminate.

A challenge such writers face is how to deal with the digit 0, which first occurs in the thirty-second place after the decimal point. One solution is to use punctuation, a full stop for example. Another is to use a ten-letter word. Some writers use longer words for two successive digits. For example, the eleven-letter word 'calculating' would stand for a 1 followed by another 1.

When I look at a sequence of numbers, my head begins to fill with colours, shapes and textures that knit together spontaneously to form a visual landscape. These are always very beautiful to me; as a child I often spent hours at a time exploring numerical landscapes in my mind. To recall each digit, I simply retrace the different shapes and textures in my head and read the numbers out of them.

For very long numbers, such as pi, I break the digits down into smaller segments. The size of each segment varies, depending on what the digits are. For example, if a number is very bright in my head and the next one is very dark, I would visualise them separately, whereas a smooth number followed by another smooth number would be remembered together. As the sequence of digits grows, my numerical landscapes become more complex and layered, until – as with pi – they are like an entire country in my mind, composed of numbers.

This is how I 'see' the first twenty digits of pi:

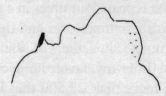

The number slopes upwards, then darkens and becomes bumpy in the middle before curving and meandering down.

And here are the first 100 digits of pi as I see them:

At the end of each segment of numbers, the landscape changes and new shapes, colours and textures appear. This process continues on and on, for as long as the sequence of digits that I am recalling.

The most famous sequence of numbers in pi is the 'Feynman point', which comprises the 762nd through 767th decimal places of pi: '. . . 999999 . . .'. It is named after the physicist Richard Feynman for his remark that he would like to memorise the digits of pi as far as that point so that when reciting them, he would be able to finish with: '. . . nine, nine, nine, nine, nine, nine, and so on.' The Feynman point is visually very beautiful to me; I see it as a deep, thick rim of dark blue light.

There is a similarly beautiful sequence of digits comprising the 19,437th through 19,453rd decimal places of pi: '. . . 99992128599999399 . . .', where the digit nine first repeats four times in a row, then very shortly afterwards five times over and then twice more again; eleven times altogether in the space of 17 decimal places. It is my favourite sequence of pi's digits in all the more than 22,500 that I learned.

I began studying pi in December 2003, having three months to learn all the digits (22,500+) needed to attempt the record. The first problem was where to find so many digits of pi: most books only gave the number to some tens or hundreds of places. The Internet proved to be the answer, though even then it took a lot of searching as most websites only listed pi to a thousand or several thousand places. Finally, Neil found the website of a Tokyo-based supercomputer which had files that stored millions of pi's digits. This, then, became our source for the record attempt.

Neil printed the numbers onto sheets of A4 paper, 1,000 digits per page, to make it convenient for me to pick up a sheet at a time and study it. The digits were further broken up into 'sentences' of 100 digits each, to make them as easily readable as possible and to mini- mise the risk that I might misread the numbers and learn some of them incorrectly.

I didn't study the sheets of numbers every day. Some days I would be too tired or restless to sit and learn anything. Other days I would gorge on the numbers, absorbing many hundreds at a single sitting. Neil noticed that when I was learning the numbers, my body became tense and agitated – I would rock backwards and forwards in my chair or pull at my lips continuously with my fingers. In those moments, he found it nearly impossible to talk or interact with me, it was as though I were in another world.

The periods of study were often short (most were an hour or less) because my concentration fluctuates a lot. I chose the quietest rooms at the back of the house in which to learn the numbers, as even the smallest sound can make it impossible for me to concentrate on what I am doing. Sometimes I put my fingers in my ears to help keep any noise out. While learning, I often walked in circles around the room with my head down and my eyes half-open, so that I wouldn't bump into things. At other times, I sat in a chair and closed my eyes completely and visualised my numerical landscapes and the many patterns and colours and textures within them.

As the public recitation was to be spoken and not written, it was important for me to practise reciting the numbers out loud to another person. Once a week, Neil would hold one or more of the sheets of numbers in front of him to check, while I stood or walked up and down and recited the growing sequence of memorised digits to him. It was an odd experience and difficult for me at first to say the numbers out loud, as they were entirely visual to me, and in the first practice recitation in front of Neil I was hesitant and made several errors. It was very frustrating and I worried about how I would cope when I would be expected to recite the entire sequence in front of a crowd of people. As always, Neil was patient and reassuring – he knew why I was finding it difficult to say the numbers out loud and encouraged me to relax and just to keep trying.

With practice, it gradually did become easier for me to recite the number continuously and my confidence began to rise as the date of the event approached. As the number of digits became larger and larger, it was not possible to recite all of them at one time in front of Neil, so we decided that I would practise reciting different parts of the number with him each week. At other times, I recited the number out loud to myself while sitting or walking around the house, until the flow of numbers became smooth and consistent.

To help with the fundraising, the charity put a donation page on the Internet that received contributions and messages of support from people all over the world. For example, one of the donations came from a class at a school in Warsaw, Poland. The charity also sent out a press release, while Neil and I collected donations from friends and family. A neighbour who heard about the event spoke to me about his own daughter's epilepsy and expressed his admiration for what I was doing. Receiving such words of support, as well as cards and emails wishing me good luck, was extremely inspiring.

At the start of the weekend of the event, Saturday 13 March, Neil drove us up to Oxford for the recitation the following day. Although I had finished learning the digits several weeks before, I was still very nervous about the prospect of reciting them in public. We stayed overnight at a guesthouse close to the museum and I tried to sleep as best I could, which wasn't easy because I kept thinking and worrying about what might happen the next day. Eventually, I fell asleep and dreamed that I was walking among my pi number landscapes – there at least I felt calm and confident.

The following morning, we both woke early. I wasn't the only nervous one as Neil complained of stomach cramps, which he knew was because he was feeling so tense about the day ahead. We ate breakfast together, then made our way to the museum. It was my first time in Oxford and I was excited to see it, a city famous for its University (the oldest in the English-speaking world) and known as the 'city of dreaming spires' in reference to the architecture of the university buildings. We drove down a series of long, narrow cobbled roads until we arrived at our destination.

The Museum of the History of Science, located in Broad Street, is the world's oldest surviving purpose-built museum building. Built in 1683, it was the first museum in the world to open to the public. Among its

collection of around 15,000 objects, dating from anti-
quity to the early twentieth century, is a wide range of
early mathematical instruments used for calculating,
astronomy, navigation, surveying and drawing.

As we drove in to the car park opposite the museum, we
could see members of staff from the museum, journalists,
cameramen and the charity's event organisers all
waiting together outside for us to arrive. Simon, the
charity's fundraising manager, walked over as I got out
from the car and shook my hand vigorously and asked
how I was feeling. I replied that I was feeling fine. I was
introduced to the other people waiting for me and then
asked to sit on the steps of the building and have some
photos taken of me. The step felt cold and damp and I
tried not to fidget too much.

Inside, the room for the recitation was long and
dusty and filled from end to end with glass cases
containing various exhibits. Against the wall on one
side was a small table and chair for me to sit at. From it,
I had a direct view of Einstein's blackboard on the wall
opposite me. A little way from my table was a longer
one, with sheets of paper filled with numbers and a
digital clock. Seated around the table were members of
the department of mathematical sciences from nearby
Oxford Brookes University, who had volunteered to be
checkers during the recitation. Their task was to monitor my recall and ensure total accuracy, checking the
numbers on the pages in front of them as I recalled the
digits out loud. The clock was to be started at the

beginning of the recitation, so that members of the public who came in and watched could see how long I had been reciting for. The event had been promoted in the local press and there were posters outside the building to encourage passers-by inside, where charity workers were ready with information booklets and buckets for any donations.

Neil was still very tense, to the point of feeling quite sick, but was determined to stay in the hall to give me his support and his presence was definitely reassuring. After posing for more photos inside the hall, I sat down at my chair and put the few things I had brought with me onto my table. There were bottles of water to drink whenever my throat felt dry and chocolate and bananas to provide me with energy throughout the recitation. As Simon called for silence, I was ready to start and he began the clock at five minutes past eleven.

And so I recited the by now very familiar opening digits of pi, the numerical landscapes in my head growing and changing as I went along. As I recited, the checkers crossed off each number as it was correctly recalled. There was a state of almost complete silence throughout the hall, except for the very occasional muffled cough or the sound of footsteps as someone moved from one side of the hall to the other. The noises did not bother me, because as I recited I could feel myself becoming absorbed within the visual flow of colours and shapes, textures and motion, until I was surrounded by my numerical landscapes. The reciting became almost melodic as each breath was filled with number upon number upon number and then I suddenly realised that I was totally calm, as I had been in my dream the night before. It took a little over ten minutes to complete the first thousand digits. I opened one of the bottles and drank some water, then continued the recitation.

Gradually, the hall began to fill with members of the public who stood several metres back from me and watched in silence as I recited. Though I had worried most of all about reciting pi in front of so many people, in the end I almost did not notice them as all of my thoughts were absorbed in the rhythmic and continuous flow of numbers. There was only one significant interruption that I can remember, when someone's mobile phone started to ring. At that point I stopped reciting and waited for the noise to stop before continuing.

The rules of the event meant that I could not talk or interact with anyone during the course of the recitation. Short, pre-arranged breaks were allowed, during which I ate some of my chocolate or a banana. To help keep my concentration during the breaks, I walked from one side of the room to the other, backwards and forwards behind my chair, with my head down looking at the floor, avoiding the gazes of the spectators. Sitting continuously in my seat while reciting was something that I found even more difficult than I had expected, as I tend to fidget a lot. While recalling the digits I would roll my head or cover it with my hands or gently rock myself with my eyes closed.

I reached 10,000 digits at quarter past one in the afternoon, just over two hours from the start of the recitation. As the hours passed, I could feel myself becoming more and more tired and I could see that the visual landscapes in my mind were becoming increasingly blurred as the fatigue started to set in. I hadn't recited all the digits together in a continuous sequence before the event and I now hoped that I would not get so tired that I would be unable to finish.

There was, in the end, only one point at which I momentarily thought I might not be able to continue. It was after reaching 16,600 digits that for just a few moments my mind went completely blank: no shapes, no colours, no textures, nothing. I hadn't ever experienced anything like it before, as though I was looking into a black hole. I closed my eyes tight and took several deep breaths, then I felt a tingling in my head and from the darkness the colours started to flow again and I continued to recite as before.

By mid-afternoon, I was finally nearing the close of my numerical journey. I felt exhausted after five hours and was glad to have the end in sight. It felt as though I had run a marathon in my head. At exactly quarter past four, my voice shaking with relief, I recited the last digits: '67657486953587' and signalled that I had finished. I had recited 22,514 digits of pi without error in a time of 5 hours and 9 minutes to set a new British and European record. The audience of spectators burst into loud applause and Simon ran over and surprised me with a hug. After giving my thanks to the checkers for monitoring the recitation throughout, I was asked to come outside for more photos and to receive my first ever glass of champagne.

The subsequent response from the media to the event was phenomenal and much greater than anything the charity or I had expected. In the weeks that followed, I gave interviews for various newspapers and radio stations, including the BBC World Service and stations in places as far away as Canada and Australia.

One of the most common questions I was asked in these interviews was: Why learn a number like pi to so many decimal places? The answer I gave then as I do now is that pi is for me an extremely beautiful and utterly unique thing. Like the Mona Lisa or a Mozart symphony, pi is its own reason for loving it.

11

Meeting Kim Peek

Amid the ensuing spate of newspaper articles and radio interviews following the success of my pi record attempt came an offer from a major TV channel in the UK to commission a one-hour documentary programme around my story, to be screened in Britain and the United States the following year. The programme makers had been impressed by the footage they had seen of me in Oxford and especially by my ability to cope well with the public and media interest in me. They were planning to go to America later in the year to film Kim Peek, the savant who was the real-life inspiration behind the *Rain Man* film character, and

believed that my ability to articulate my own experiences as a savant would make me an accessible point of
focus for the programme. Besides meeting Kim face to
face, there would also be the opportunity for me to
meet some of the world's leading scientists and researchers in savant syndrome, both in the US and
Britain. It seemed like the opportunity of a lifetime.

I agreed to take part, though I was very anxious. I had
not been outside the UK for five years (nor in that time
scarcely even outside my home town) and the prospect
of several weeks far away from home, travelling and
filming, daunted me. I worried whether I would be able
to cope with the demanding travel schedule without my
usual routines or counting rituals. I had never been to
America before (though I could recite the dates, middle
names and party affiliation of every president from
McKinley onwards) and did not know how I would
find it: what if it was too big, too flashy, too noisy for me?
What if I felt overwhelmed and panicked in this vast
country an ocean away from home?

The thought of constantly being on the move, from
day to day and location to location, was the biggest
concern for my family, Neil and me. Though supportive, they urged me to talk things over with the production team. In the conversations I had with the team I
was reassured that they would ensure I was never left
alone in a public place (where I might get lost) and that
the filming would not be intrusive, but would capture
events as they happened.

The schedule set by the team was ambitious: we were to zigzag from coast to coast over the period of two weeks with points of call en route as diverse as San Diego, California and Salt Lake City, Utah. The programme makers very quickly came up with the working title *Brainman* – a pun on the Dustin Hoffman film – that though at first I disliked, over time I grew to accept.

I met the crew for the first time a week before the trip in July 2004. They were friendly and helped put me at ease. The cameraman, Toby, was the same age as me. Everyone was excited – this was a completely different kind of programme for the crew and they did not quite know what to expect. I was excited too, in part because they were excited and I take a lot of my emotional cues from the actions and reactions of those around me. I also felt happy inside; a new adventure was beginning.

I finished packing my bags the evening before the flight: one coat, two pairs of shoes, four sweaters, six pairs of shorts and trousers, eight t-shirts, eleven pairs of socks and underwear, a fresh tube of toothpaste, electric toothbrush, cleanser, essential oils, shower gel and shampoo. Neil purchased a mobile phone for me so we could stay in touch while I was away. His work prevented him from coming with me. I kept the phone in my right pocket and my passport, ticket and wallet in my left.

Neil drove me to the airport and hugged me before I entered the terminal. This would be the first time in three and a half years that we would be apart. Even so, I did not realise that I should show any emotion and the hug startled me. Inside the terminal building there were lots of people with luggage. They were moving around me on all sides and I began to feel anxious, so I started to count the people in the queues and felt better. The crew had already arrived and we eventually made our way over to the waiting area and then on to the plane.

It was a typically warm and clear summer day and I watched from my seat as the blue sky disappeared below clouds as we soared high into the air. An announcement from the pilot told us that the flight time was eleven hours to Los Angeles International Airport. Whenever I am given a time estimate, I visualise it in my head as a length of dough across a table, which I picture as being an hour long. For example, I am able to understand how long a thirty-minute walk will take by imagining a piece of dough rolled out to halfway across my mental table. But eleven hours was an unprecedentedly long period of time for me and I found it impossible to picture in my mind. This made me very nervous and I squeezed my eyes shut very tight, then opened them slowly and looked down at my feet until I felt calmer.

I like to prepare myself mentally for an upcoming event, to rehearse the different possibilities or permutations in my mind because of the way I become uncomfortable when something happens suddenly or unexpectedly. I knew at some point on board a steward would approach and ask me something (about my choice of meal, for example) so I pictured the steward standing over me and talking to me. In my mind, I imagined myself calm and answering without difficulty.

My hands hovered continuously around my pockets, checking for the hundredth time that my phone was in my right pocket and my passport and wallet in my left. As I heard the rattling of trolleys approaching my seat I could feel myself becoming more and more tense and vigilant. I listened carefully to some of the stewards' conversations with the other passengers so that I knew what the steward would say to me. I had my choice ready in my mind: chicken and dumpling stew. The trolley came and went without a hitch. And I'd made a good choice.

I remained too anxious to sleep during the flight. Instead, I read the in-flight magazine and listened to music through the plastic headphones provided. As we eventually came in to land I could not help but feel an unmistakable sense of achievement: I had made it. My head hurt and my arms and legs were stiff, but I was in America.

Outside, the weather was clear and warmer than it had been in London. I waited while the director organised a hire car. After it came, the crew piled the luggage and many boxes full of camera and recording equipment into the back. It was like watching a game of Tetris. After several attempts, they finally managed to make everything fit. The drive took us to San Diego and a hotel next to the sea. Though exhausted, I was told we were due for an early start the next day. Inside my hotel room I brushed my teeth methodically, washed my face with my usual (five) number of splashes of water at the sink and set the alarm for 4.30 a.m. before climbing into bed and falling – immediately – into a deep sleep.

As the alarm screeched into life I jumped up and covered my ears with my hands. My head was hurting and I was unused to the sound of an alarm clock. I fumbled with one hand until I found the right switch and brought the room back to silence. It was still dark outside. I brushed my teeth for exactly two minutes and then showered. I did not like that everything in the room was different. The showerhead was larger, the water felt heavier as it fell onto my head and the texture of the towels felt strange. Once dry, I rushed into my clothes; they at least seemed and fitted how I knew they would. With considerable trepidation, I made my way slowly out of the door and down a flight of stairs to the breakfast room below. I waited for Toby to arrive, a familiar face, before sitting down and beginning to eat. I ate a muffin with some tea and after the others had come down and finished eating we clambered into the car and drove out to a large number of tall buildings with sparkling windows. We were to meet the acclaimed neurologist Professor Ramachandran and his team at California's Center for Brain Studies.

The scientists came out to greet us as we arrived. We were taken to the Professor's office, past corridors that shone with the bright sunlight that poured in from the windows fitted all along one side. The office was large, darker than the corridors that led to it, with walls filled with tightly-knit rows of books, and a heavy-set table covered with plastic models of brains and sprawling sheets of paper. I was beckoned over to a chair, opposite the professor and one of his team members.

When the professor spoke, his voice boomed. In fact everything about him seemed somehow loud – his big, round eyes and thick curly black hair and moustache. I remember thinking how large his outstretched hands appeared to me. His enthusiasm was obvious and somehow helped to put me at ease. Though I felt nervous, there was a shiver of excitement too.

I was asked to do some calculations in my head while the professor's assistant checked my answers with a calculator. My head was still hurting from the jet lag, but fortunately I was still able to do the scientists' sums. They then read out a list of numbers and asked me to say whether each was prime or not. I got every one right. I explained how I saw the numbers in my head as colours, shapes and textures. The professor seemed both intrigued and impressed.

At lunch, the professor's assistant, a young man called Shai with jet-black hair and big, round eyes like the professor's, escorted me to a canteen on the center's campus. Shai was fascinated by my descriptions of how I visualised numbers and the answers to different calculations in my head. Later, I was called to another room where I met another of Professor Ramachandran's team members, Ed. Shai and Ed wanted to know more about the specific visual experiences I had for different numbers. It was hard to find the words to describe them so I picked up a pen and started to draw the shapes of the numbers they asked about on a white board. The scientists were stunned. They had not anticipated that my experiences were as complex as they now appeared, nor that I would be able to demonstrate them in such detail.

The scientists' reaction took everyone by surprise. They asked the director if they could have more time to study some of my specific abilities and my visual experiences of numbers. The director made a call to the producer in London who agreed.

The following day, with the cameras rolling, I was asked to go back over my descriptions and drawings of different numbers from the previous day. I walked over to the white board and gradually covered it with drawings and illustrations of how I saw various numbers and calculated sums in my head using my synaesthetic shapes. I was even asked to model some of the numbers in play-dough.

Then I was asked to study a computer screen filled with digits from the number pi while my fingers were wired up to a galvanic skin response meter. The scientists had secretly substituted sixes for nines at random points in the sequence and were interested to see whether the changes would trigger anything on the meter's reading. As I looked at the numbers on the screen I started to feel uncomfortable and grimaced a lot, because I could see parts of my numerical land-scapes were broken up as though they had been van-dalised. The galvanic meter measured significant fluctuations, indicating that I did have a physiological response to the numbers being altered. The scientists, especially Shai, were fascinated.

Sometimes people ask me if I mind being a guinea pig for the scientists. I have no problem with it because I know that I am helping them to understand the human brain better, which is something that will benefit everyone. It is also gratifying for me to learn more about myself, and the way in which my mind works.

As my time with the scientists drew rapidly to a close on what was now an even tighter schedule than before, Shai asked if he could drive me over to the nearby cliffs to look out at the sea and watch the gliders floating in the sky above. He was keen to spend some time with me away from the crew and cameras. We walked together along the cliffs and he asked about my feelings for different numbers, making notes with a pad and pen he had brought along specially. My answers seemed to excite him even more. 'Do you know, you're a once in a lifetime opportunity for scientists,' he said matter-of-factly, but I did not know how to answer. I liked Shai and promised to stay in touch, which we do to this day by email.

Our next stop was Las Vegas, Nevada's 'City of Dreams' and the undisputed epicentre of the gambling world. The production had been keen to demonstrate some of my abilities in a 'light-hearted' televisual approach, and this would be that stage, taking a page out of the famous sequence from *Rain Man*.

I had mixed feelings about this proposed sequence in the programme. The last thing I wanted to do was to trivialise my abilities or reinforce the erroneous stereotype that all autistic people were like the *Rain Man* character. At the same time, I understood that the programme needed to have some fun and visual sequences to cut between the more serious scientific ones. I enjoyed playing cards with friends but had never stepped inside a casino before in my life. Curiosity was enough to help sway me.

The heat in the Nevada air was incredible, like having a hair dryer turned up to maximum and continuously blown straight at you. Even dressed in a light cotton t-shirt and shorts, my body was quickly soaked in sweat as we waited for the hire car to take us on to the next hotel. The journey was thankfully swift and we were all grateful for the hotel lobby's air conditioning. Driving past the massive, gaudy buildings had been a nauseating experience and the sense of relief was palpable.

The sight that met us on our arrival at the hotel's

reception quickly mitigated any excitement we might have felt. The producer, having found it remarkably difficult to find a casino willing to allow television cameras in to film, had in the end settled for an establishment downtown. It was much smaller than its more famous casino cousins, and had enthusiastically embraced the idea and even provided our rooms free of charge. Our initial impression, however, was not good. The carpet was dirty and there was a persistent, stale smell throughout the lobby. It did not help that it took a long time, more than an hour, for the staff to organise our rooms.

However, once given our keys we found the rooms surprisingly spacious and comfortable. As night fell, I was taken down to the car and filmed as we drove along Vegas's famous strip, bleached from all directions by dazzling casino lights. I clasped my hands tightly together and felt my body becoming tense and rigid, uncomfortable at being surrounded by so many stimulating sensations. Fortunately the drive did not last long. We ate together at a nearby restaurant before going early to bed.

Next morning, the crew were busy for a long time setting up in a quiet section of the blackjack tables' area before coming to collect me. The casino's management had organised a large quantity of 'play money' chips for us to use for the sequence. I met the casino's owner and was introduced to the dealer, who quickly explained the rules of the game to me.

Blackjack is one of the most popular of the gambling card games; it is also known as 'vingt-et-un' or 'twenty-one'. The object of the game is to bet on each hand as to whether the player's cards will beat the dealer's hand without exceeding twenty-one. An ace can count as either one or eleven, while face cards (jacks, queens, kings) score ten.

At the start of each hand, initial bets are placed and the dealer deals two cards to each player and himself. One of the two dealer's cards is left face down. A face card plus an ace is called a 'blackjack' and results in an immediate win for the holder. Otherwise, the dealer gives each player the option of asking for more cards ('hitting') or staying with his current total ('standing' or 'holding'). If a player goes over twenty-one ('busts') he loses. Following the decisions of the players, the dealer reveals the hidden card and decides whether or not to draw additional cards. If he has a score lower than seventeen, he must draw a further card or cards until reaching a minimum total value of seventeen. If the dealer busts, all the remaining players win.

The practice of card counting is well-known in blackjack and consists of the player mentally tracking the sequence of played cards in an attempt to gain a small advantage over the dealer, increasing a bet when the count is good (for example, when the remaining decks contain many face cards) and decreasing when it is bad. In its simplest form, card counting involves assigning a positive or negative value to each card; low-value cards, such as 2 and 3, are given a positive value, while tens are given a negative value. The counter then mentally keeps a running tally of the point values as each card is dealt and makes regular adjustments to the overall count, taking into account the approximate number of cards still left to be dealt.

Card counting is not easy and even highly skilled practitioners only gain around 1% by using this method. Casinos will often ban those they suspect of card counting from their tables. Our table used an eight-deck shoe, meaning that there were 416 cards in play, a number large enough to minimise any possible counting advantage.

Casinos are noisy and distracting environments in which to play and one of the biggest challenges for me was trying to concentrate. As I sat on my stool opposite the dealer I focused on the decks of cards, watching intently as they were individually opened, shuffled and stacked ahead of the start of the game. The cameras around me attracted onlookers and I quickly had a crowd encircle me as I played.

I was to play for a pre-set period of time. The casino had specially reserved the table so that I was the only player. It was the dealer versus me. Wanting to develop a feel for the game, I started by making simple judgements based on the cards displayed in each hand: I would 'stand' if dealt a 10 and 8 and 'hit' if given a 3 and 9 (except where the dealer showed a 4, 5 or 6, in which case I stood), a technique known as 'basic strategy'.

Even when the player uses basic strategy optimally, the dealer still has a statistical advantage. Over time my stack of chips became increasingly depleted. My feel for how the cards were playing, however, was a lot better than at the start; I was making my decisions more quickly and feeling more comfortable at the table. I made a snap decision to play instinctively, going on how I was experiencing the flow of numbers in my head as a rolling visual landscape with peaks and troughs. When my mental numerical landscape peaked, I would bet more aggressively than when it ebbed.

A change occurred; I began to win more and more individual hands. I relaxed and began to enjoy the game much more than I had been. At a key point I was dealt a pair of 7s with the dealer showing a 10. Basic strategy says to hit. Instead I went with my instinct and split the pair, doubling my original bet. The dealer drew a third card, which was also a 7. I asked if I could split this 7. The dealer was surprised – this is extremely unusual play against a dealer's 10. The card was split and I now had three hands of 7, my original bet trebled, against a 10. The audience of onlookers behind me were audibly tutting. One man loudly remarked: 'What's he doing splitting 7s against a 10?' The dealer proceeded to deal out further cards on each of the three 7s – the first totalled twenty-one. Then more cards for the second-hand: another twenty-one. Finally came the third of the 7s, and once again a winning total of twenty-one. Three consecutive twenty-ones in a single hand against the dealer. In one fell blow I had made up my losses and beaten the house.

I was still glad to leave Las Vegas. It was too hot, too crowded, with too many flashing lights. The only time I had felt comfortable was among the cards. I was feeling increasingly homesick and after returning to the hotel phoned Neil from my room, bursting into tears at the sound of his voice. He told me I was doing fine and should carry on. He was proud of me. I was not to know then that the most important and special episode in the entire trip was just ahead of me.

We flew into Salt Lake City, capital of the state of Utah and home to the Mormon religion, the following day. It was a short drive from the hotel to the city's public library. The building was extraordinary: six-storey curving, transparent walls covering 240,000 square feet and containing more than half a million books, with shops and services at ground level, reading galleries above and a 300-seat auditorium. With my abiding love of books and memories of the years spent reading for hours in my small local libraries every day, this seemed like paradise to me.

The huge space was infused with daylight and I felt the familiar tingle of tranquillity inside me. Libraries had always had the power to make me feel at peace. There were no crowds, only small pockets of indivi-duals reading or moving from shelf to shelf or desk to desk. There was no sudden loud outburst of noise, just the gentle flicking of pages or the intimate chatter between friends and colleagues. I had never seen or been in any library quite like this before; it really seemed to me like the enchanted palace of a fairy tale.

I was asked to sit on a bench on the ground floor and wait, so I counted the rows of books and the people as they walked quietly by. I could have sat there for hours. The director came and collected me and we rode the elevator to the second floor. Here there were rows upon rows of books for as far as the eye could see. An elderly man approached and shook my hand. He introduced himself as Fran Peek, father and full-time carer of his son, Kim.

Kim Peek is a miracle. When he was born in 1951, doctors told his parents that he would never walk or learn and that they should put him in an institution. Kim was born with an enlarged head and a water blister inside his skull that damaged the left hemisphere, the side of the brain involved in such critical areas as speech and language. A 1988 scan by neuroscientists found that he had no corpus callosum, the membrane separating the brain's two hemispheres. Yet he was able to read at sixteen months and completed the high school curriculum by age fourteen.

Kim has memorised a vast amount of information from more than a dozen subjects over the years, ranging from history and dates to literature, sports, geography and music. He can read two pages of a book simultaneously, one with each eye, with near perfect

retention. Kim has read more than 9,000 books altogether and can recall their entire content. He is also a
gifted calendrical calculator.

In 1984, Kim and his father met producer and
screenwriter Barry Morrow at a conference meeting
of the Association of Retarded Citizens in Arlington,
Texas. The result was the movie *Rain Man*. Dustin
Hoffman spent the day with Kim and was so awed by
his abilities that he urged Fran to share his son with the
world. Since that time, Kim and his father have criss-
crossed the US and talked to more than a million
people.

This was to be a moment I had long waited for; it
would be the first time in my life that I had met and
spoken with another savant. Fran had told his son who
I was and why we were coming to meet them. The
choice of the city's public library for our meeting was a
no-brainer; for both Kim and myself libraries are a
special place, full of quiet, light, space and order.

After meeting Fran I was introduced to Kim. Standing close to his father, Kim was a heavy-set, middle-
aged figure with a mop of greying hair and piercing,
inquisitive eyes. He quickly held my arms and stood
very close to me. 'Give him your birth date,' suggested
Fran. '31 January 1979,' I said. 'You turn sixty-five on
a Sunday,' replied Kim. I nodded and asked for his
birth date. '11 November 1951,' he replied. I smiled
broadly: 'You were born on a Sunday!' Kim's face lit
up and I knew that we had connected.

Fran had a surprise for me: the Oscar won by *Rain Man*'s screenwriter Barry Morrow which Morrow generously gave the Peeks to take on their speaking tours. I held the statuette carefully in both hands; it was much heavier than it looked. I was asked to sit with Fran and talk about Kim's childhood, so we walked over to a corner with comfortable leather chairs and sat while Kim was given a book to read. Fran spoke with passion about the reaction of the doctors to his young son's problems: 'We were told to put him in an institution and forget about him.' A brain surgeon even offered to lobotomise Kim to make it easier to institutionalise him.

I wanted to know more about Kim's life today and asked Fran to describe a typical day's routine. 'Kim speaks to his mother on the phone every morning and he comes here every day and reads for several hours. In the evenings we go visit an elderly neighbour of ours. Kim reads to her.'

I asked about Kim's speaking tours. 'We always travel together and never ask for any money. We visit places like schools, colleges and hospitals. Kim can tell them almost anything they want to know: dates, names, statistics, zip codes, you name it. The audience asks him all sorts of questions and he always comes out with so much information, more than I ever knew he knew. He hardly ever gets stuck for an answer. His message is this: "You don't have to be disabled to be different, because everybody's different."'

We finished the interview and I was able to walk with Kim alone around the different shelves of the library. Kim held my hand as we walked. 'You're a savant like me, Daniel,' he said excitedly and he squeezed my hand. As we walked among the shelves I noticed that Kim would pause briefly and take a book from the shelf, flick through a few pages as if already familiar with its contents, and return it. He would sometimes murmur a name or date out loud as he read. Every book dealt with non-fiction topics; novels did not seem to interest him. It was something else that we had in common.

'What do you like doing here most, Kim?' I asked him and without saying a word he took me over to a section with rows of thick, red leather-clad books. They were phone directories for every town in Salt Lake City. Kim pulled one off the shelf and sat himself down at a nearby desk. He had a notebook and pen with him and proceeded to copy several names and numbers from the directory into his book. I watched and asked him if he liked numbers too; he nodded slowly, absorbed in his notes.

I sat with Kim and remembered that Fran had told me Kim enjoyed being given questions related to historical dates and figures. History was one of Kim's favourite topics. 'What year did Victoria become Queen of England?' I asked. '1837,' replied Kim in an instant. 'How old would Winston Churchill be if he were alive today?' '130'. 'And what day of the week would his birthday fall on this year?' 'It would be a Tuesday, the last day of November.'

With Fran and the crew's supervision we were then taken down to the library's ground floor where Kim pointed to the different rows of shelves and explained which books they contained. We walked out into bright mid-afternoon sun and then stood, Kim once more clasping my hands in his. Standing close to me, he looked into my eyes and said: 'One day you'll be as great as I am.' It was the best compliment I had ever received.

I agreed to meet Kim and Fran later that evening for supper at a local restaurant. Kim recounted his memory of meeting Dustin Hoffman and Hoffman's amazement at Kim's abilities and warm character. Both father and son emphasised the importance of continuing to share Kim's abilities and his message of respect for difference with as many people as possible.

We left Kim and Fran in Salt Lake City with considerable reluctance. Each member of the crew said how much they had taken away from the experience of meeting Kim and his father. Their story of unconditional love and of dedication and perseverance in the face of adversity was extremely inspiring. For me, it had been a simply unforgettable experience. Kim reminded me of how fortunate I was, in spite of my own difficulties, to be able to live the sort of independent life that he cannot. It was equally a joy to find someone who loved books and facts and figures as much as I did.

As we flew home, I was left with several thoughts. Kim and I had much in common, but most important of all was the sense of connection I think we both felt during our time together. Our lives had in many ways been very different and yet somehow we shared this special, rarefied bond. It had helped to bring us together and on that day we reminded one another of the extraordinary value of friendship. I had been moved by the enthusiasm with which he and his father had welcomed me and with which they had openly and candidly shared their story. Kim's special gift is not only his brain, but also his heart, his humanity, his ability to touch the lives of others in a truly unique way. Meeting Kim Peek was one of the happiest moments of my life.

12

Reykjavík, New York, Home

After my return to the UK, the programme makers had one last challenge for me: to learn a new language from scratch in one week in front of the cameras. They had spent several months researching various possibilities, before finally settling on Icelandic – an inflected language, largely unchanged since the thirteenth century and comparable to Old English, and spoken today by around 300,000 people. Here is a written example, to give an idea of what it looks like:

Mörður hér maður er kallaður var gígja. Hann var sonur Sighvats hins rauða. Hann bjó á Velli á

Rangárvöllum. Hann var ríkur höfðingi og mála-
fylgjumaður mikill og svo mikill lögmaður að engir
þóttu löglegir dómar dæmdir nema hann væri við.
Hann átti dóttur eina er Unnur hét. Hún var væn
kona og kurteis og vel að sér og þótti sá bestur
kostur á Rangárvöllum.

There was a man named Mord whose surname
was Fiddle; he was the son of Sigvat the Red, and he
dwelt at the 'Vale' in the Rangrivervales. He was a
mighty chief, and a great taker up of suits, and so
great a lawyer that no judgments were thought
lawful unless he had a hand in them. He had an
only daughter, named Unna. She was a fair, cour-
teous, and gifted woman, and that was thought the
best match in all the Rangrivervales.

Excerpted from *Brennu-Njáls Saga (The Saga of
Burnt Njál)*, Iceland's most famous saga, dating
from the thirteenth century.

Icelandic is considered a very complex and difficult
language to learn; for example, there are no less than
twelve different words for each of the numbers from
one to four, depending on the context of the sentence.
Icelandic nouns have one of three genders: masculine,
feminine and neuter. Adjectives change according to
the gender of the noun they describe: *Gunnar er
svangur* ('Gunnar is strong') but *Helga er svöng* ('Helga
is strong') where Gunnar is male and Helga female. In

addition, Icelanders do not borrow words from other languages as do the English, but create their own words for modern things: *tölva* for 'computer' and *sími* for 'telephone' (from an Old Icelandic word meaning 'thread').

In September the programme makers' choice of language was finally revealed to me in a package sent to my home. It contained a pocket dictionary, a children's book, two grammar books and several newspapers. The production had decided for budgetary reasons to have only four days in Iceland, instead of the one week that had originally been planned, and for this reason the language learning material had been forwarded to my home several days ahead of the trip. However, there was a serious difficulty: the dictionary provided was very small, so it was almost impossible to begin decoding the texts provided by the production. I was also unhappy that there would be only four days instead of the seven originally planned in Iceland, since the culmination of the language challenge was going to be a live television interview in Reykjavík conducted entirely in Icelandic. To complete the challenge successfully, I needed as much exposure to the spoken language as possible.

The situation being as it was, I did the best I could with the material I had. I learned common phrases and vocabulary from the grammar books and practised building my own sentences from the word patterns I was able to pick out from the various texts. One of the books came with a CD, so I tried to listen to it to get a sense of accent and pronunciation, but it was very difficult for me to concentrate because of the way my brain tunes in and out while listening. With another person I can listen very intently, making a special effort to sustain my level of concentration throughout, but I find this much harder to do when listening to a CD, maybe because there isn't the requirement to make such a big effort to stay continuously engaged. As a result of these difficulties, I was beginning to feel very disheartened as the day of the flight arrived.

It was time to say goodbye to Neil again, though at least it would only be for a few days. I was collected by taxi and driven to the airport where I met the film crew. Fortunately it was quiet and there were few people walking around. I had brought the books with me, but hoped to receive better learning materials once we arrived in Iceland. The flight was not long and I spent most of the time looking out of the window or reading through the stories in the Icelandic children's book.

Iceland is one of the smallest countries in the world, with a population of little over a quarter of a million. It is situated in the North Atlantic, just south of the Arctic Circle. Located on a geological hot spot on the mid-Atlantic ridge, the island is extremely geologically active. It has many volcanoes and geysers, and geothermal power heats many Icelanders' homes. The nation's literacy rate is 100% and poetry and literature are popular. More books, magazines and periodicals are published per capita in Iceland than anywhere else in the world.

Upon arrival at Keflavík airport it was a bus ride to Iceland's largest city, the capital, Reykjavík (with a population of just over 110,000 it has the nickname *Stærsta smáborg í heimi* – 'the biggest small city in the world').

It was near the close of summer, though the weather was still calm: the air was chilly and fresh, but not bitterly cold. The bus had long, shiny windows running down each side and looking out as we rode we saw large swathes of silver-grey clouds hanging in the sky and underneath a stream of stark, metallic blue landscape in the distance. As we neared Reykjavík I could see the daylight begin to soften and scatter and I closed my eyes and counted to myself, in Icelandic: *einn, tveir, þrír, fjórir* . . .

At the hotel I had my first meeting with my Icelandic tutor Sigriður, though she said to call her 'Sirrý' for short. Sirrý worked with foreign students as a tutor at the local university, but said she had never heard of anyone trying to learn Icelandic in so short a space of time and was doubtful that it could be done. In a holdall Sirrý carried lots of reading materials for us to study together. Whenever an opportunity arose, we opened up the books and I read the pages out loud so she could check my pronunciation and help with any words I did not understand.

The large amount of reading helped me to develop an intuitive sense of the language's grammar. One of the things I noticed was that a lot of the words seemed to grow in length the further along they appeared in a sentence. For example, the word *bók* ('book') is often longer when used at the start of a sentence: '*Bókin er skrifuð á íslensku* ('the book is written in Icelandic') and longer still at the end: *Ég er nýbúinn að lesa bókina* ('I have just finished reading the book'). Another example is the word *borð* ('table'): *Borðið er stórt og þungt* ('the table is big and heavy') and *Orðabókin var á borðinu* ('the dictionary was on the table'). The spatial location of the word in the sentence helped me to know the grammatical form it would likely take.

The time pressure proved the toughest part of the challenge. A lot of the little time I had to study was spent in a car being driven around several different locations for filming – a problem made even worse by the fact that Sirrý was prone to carsickness. There was, of course, an upside to being taken to visit many different places; Iceland is a visually stunning place and it was an opportunity for me to absorb the atmosphere, something that would have been impossible to do in a class or hotel room.

We spent a day at Gullfoss, meaning 'the golden waterfall'. Situated in the glacial river Hvita, the enormous white cascade drops 32 metres into a narrow canyon, 70 metres deep and 2.5 kilometres long. Viewed from nearby, the fine drizzle continuously thrown up into the moisture-filled air resembled how I see the number eighty-nine in my head. This sensation was not unique. Standing out of the rain in a small, dingy wind-hewn cave close by, I felt as though I had climbed inside the dark hollowness of the number six. Even the undulating curves of faraway mountains reminded me of numerical sequences. It was then that I felt most at home in Iceland.

A trip to thermal fields in the Haukadalur valley provided the opportunity to view Iceland's famous erupting geysers up close. The word 'geyser' comes from the Icelandic verb *gjósa* meaning 'to gush'. They are a rare phenomenon – only around 1,000 exist worldwide. Geyser activity is caused by surface water gradually seeping down through fissures and collecting in caverns. The trapped water is heated by surrounding volcanic rock at a temperature of around 200 degrees Centigrade, causing it to expand into steam and force its way up and out. Eventually the remaining water in the geyser cools back to below boiling point and the eruption ends; heated surface water begins seeping back into the reservoir and the whole cycle starts over again.

Watching the geyser erupt was fascinating. At first the turquoise water begins to boil, then large bubbles form and burst, pulling the steaming water upwards. The eruption itself is sudden and violent, producing a thick, soaring column of glistening water ten or more metres in height. The air around the geyser is permeated with the smell of sulphur, like rotten eggs, which fortunately is carried away on the wind.

Travelling for long periods at a time between filming was very tiring and food breaks were always welcome. While the crew tucked into hamburgers and fries, I sampled traditional Icelandic dishes such as *kjötsúpa* (lamb soup) and *plokkfiskur* (a kind of fish hash). As much as possible, I conversed entirely in Icelandic with Sirrý, while making notes in a large, black notebook I carried around with me at all times.

The culmination of the challenge came with a live television interview on the popular current affairs programme *Kastljós* ('spotlight'). I was nervous but also confident before the interview, though I had no idea exactly what questions the interviewers would ask me. For nearly a quarter of an hour I talked with the two presenters entirely in Icelandic, in front of an audience of hundreds of thousands. It was an eerie experience to sit in front of cameras and converse in a language I had only been acquainted with for the past week. Even stranger was that I was understood completely. As the week had passed, watching and listening to various Icelanders conversing in their native tongue, it had seemed so easy and so natural to them, as though they were breathing Icelandic. In contrast, my speech was slower and more laboured. I explained to the interviewers: '*Ég er með islensku asma*' ('I have Icelandic asthma').

There were other interviews with the local media in Reykjavík and an appearance on Iceland's main breakfast television show; the interview also being conducted in Icelandic. On that programme, Sirrý also appeared with me and was very complimentary about how well she thought I had done in the week that I had been studying the language. Sirrý also gave an interview in English for the documentary programme, in which she said that she had never before had a student like me and that I was 'not human'! I was very grateful to her, not least because her help and encouragement had been invaluable to me.

Returning from Reykjavík at the close of filming the documentary I had the opportunity to reflect on just how far I had come. Only a few years before it would have seemed impossible that I would be able to live such an independent life: to fly to and travel around a country as huge as the United States, meet all sorts of people and visit all kinds of places and have the confidence to share my innermost thoughts and experiences with the world. The visit to Iceland too had been both amazing and moving and I had felt privileged that the Icelandic people had embraced me so warmly and enthusiastically. It was the strangest thing: the very same abilities that had set me apart from my peers as a child and adolescent, and isolated me from them, had actually helped me to connect with other people in adulthood and to make new friends. It had been an incredible few months for me, and it wasn't over yet.

★   ★   ★

Early one morning the following spring I received a phone call telling me that I had been invited to appear on an upcoming edition of the *Late Show with David Letterman*. The arrangements had been made through Discovery's Science Channel, which had broadcast *Brainman* for the first time several weeks before in the US. The reaction to the programme had been very positive, including a detailed review in the *New York Times*. Although I had never seen the Letterman show before, I had heard of it and knew that it was long-running and popular. The Science Channel's team had agreed to cover the costs of the trip to New York for the day's recording and a timetable had already been organised for me. There was only one catch: I had to fly out that afternoon as the interview was set to take place the next day.

It was fortunate that Neil was working from home and agreed to help me pack and take me to the airport. The necessary reservations were promptly booked on-line for me, so that all I needed to do was to get ready and go. It was a good thing that everything happened so suddenly, as I had no time to feel anxious and instead had to concentrate fully on routine matters, such as getting myself washed and dressed and my bag packed. In the car on the way to the airport, Neil tried to help me stay calm by telling me to enjoy the experience and just be myself.

The seat on the plane was big and comfortable and I was able to sleep for most of the time, which helped me a lot. Upon touchdown at JFK airport, I followed the other passengers out and through numerous passages until we arrived at the long queues for security and passport control. When it was my turn I walked up to the booth and handed over my passport. The man on the other side of the glass asked how long I was planning to stay in America and I replied: 'Two days'. Surprised, he said 'Only two days?' and I nodded.

He looked steadily at me for a moment, then returned my passport and waved me through. After collecting my bag I walked on to arrivals and saw a man holding a sign with my name on it. I had been told that a driver would be waiting for me once I arrived at JFK, so I walked up to him and he took my bag and we went to the car, which was long and black and very shiny. I was driven to a hotel on Manhattan's Central Park South and dropped off. Not long ago I would have been terrified at the idea of entering a hotel by myself and trying to find my way around all the different numbered rooms, trying not to end up desperately lost. By this time, though, I was so used to hotels that it wasn't a problem. I collected my keys, walked up the stairs to my room and went to bed.

The next morning I met with a representative of the Science Channel team called Beth. It was her task to make sure I was dressed appropriately for the show (colours, nothing white and no stripes, for example) and to make me feel as calm and comfortable as possible ahead of the taping. We walked together down a series of long, busy streets to the Ed Sullivan Theater, a radio and television studio located at 1697 Broadway, and the *Late Show*'s home for the past twelve years. After receiving my security pass, I was greeted by the programme's production staff and told the timetable for the day's episode. I asked if I could be shown around the set, so that I would be comfortable with walking out onto it during the actual taping later that afternoon. It was only a short walk from backstage and a single step up to the main platform where I would shake David's hand and sit down. The seat was large and soft, but the studio itself was very cold; I was told that David insists on a room temperature of just 58 degrees Fahrenheit. I just hoped I would not shiver too much on the show.

There was time for lunch back at the hotel before returning to the studio for the taping at 4.30 p.m. I was ushered into a small room from where I watched the opening segment of the show on a television set on the wall, before being taken to the makeup room. The bristles on the brush felt soft and soothing on my skin and I felt surprisingly relaxed as I was taken down to the set and shown where to stand while the show went to a commercial break. Then I heard David announce me to the audience and I received a signal from the floor manager to walk on. Following the preparations from earlier in the day, I remembered to keep my head up as I stepped out and shook David's hand before sitting down. I reminded myself to maintain eye contact throughout the interview. The audience were far enough back from the lights on set that it wasn't possible to see them, only hear them. This was good for me, because it gave me the feeling that David was the only person I was talking to. He started seriously, asking me about my autism and the seizures I had had as a child and even complimented me on my social skills, at which point the audience began to applaud. From that moment on I did not feel anxious at all. When I started to describe my pi record, David interrupted and said how much he liked pie and the audience laughed. He also asked me what day of the week he had been born on and gave me his date of birth: 12 April 1947. I told him that he had been born on a Saturday and that he would reach his sixty-fifth birthday in 2012 on a Thursday. The audience clapped loudly. As the interview came to a close, David shook my hand firmly and everyone backstage applauded as I walked past. Beth congratulated me and said how calm and collected I had appeared on the television screen. This experience showed me more than any other that I really was now able to make my way in the world, to do things for myself that most people take for granted such as travel at very short notice, stay alone at a hotel or walk a busy street without feeling overwhelmed by the different sights and sounds and smells all around. I felt elated by the thought that all my efforts had not been in vain, but had taken me to a point beyond my wildest dreams.

★　　★　　★

The *Brainman* documentary first aired in the UK in May 2005 and attracted record viewing figures. Since then, it has been shown in or sold to more than forty countries worldwide, from Switzerland to South Korea. I regularly receive emails and letters from individuals who have watched the programme and been touched or inspired by it, and it is exciting to think that my story has helped so many people.

The reaction of my family to the programme was also very positive. My father told me that he is very proud of what I have been able to accomplish. Since a recent fall left him partially disabled he has lived in specially-equipped accommodation, where he is able to receive constant medical care and support, near the family home. Neil and I drive up to London to visit him regularly. As he has got older, my father's mental health has stabilised and he has even used his experiences to contribute articles to a local support group's newsletter.

I did not always feel a strong emotional connection towards my parents or brothers and sisters when I was growing up, and did not at the time experience this as any kind of absence because they were simply not a part of my world. Things are different now: I am aware of how much my family love me and how much they have done for me over the years, and as I have got older the relationship between myself and my family has continued to improve. I think falling in love helped me to come a lot closer to all my feelings, not just for

Neil but also for my family and friends, and to accept them. I have a good relationship with my mother; we talk on the phone regularly and I enjoy our conversations. She continues to play a very important and supportive role in my life, encouraging and reassuring me as she has always done.

Most of my brothers and sisters are now young adults, like me. I didn't mix much with them as a child, but as adults we have gradually grown a lot closer and I have learned a lot more about each of them. The sibling closest to me in age, my brother Lee, works as a railway supervisor and is something of a computer addict. My mother complains that he spends all of his time when he is not working sitting in front of a computer screen.

My sister Claire is in her final year at university in York studying English Literature and Philosophy. Like me, she has a strong interest in words and language and is planning to become a schoolteacher after completing her education.

Steven, my second brother, continues to require a lot of help from the family because of his Asperger's. He takes medication for depression, which is a common issue for individuals on the autistic spectrum. Like me, he walks in circles whenever he is thinking very deeply about something; there is even a well-trodden circle in my family's garden where he has walked round and round so often. Steven is a keen musician with a particular fondness for stringed instruments. He has taught himself to play both the guitar and the Greek lute. He also has an encyclopaedic knowledge of his favourite music group, the Red Hot Chilli Peppers. Sometimes my parents complain about Steven's dress sense, because he wears very bright colours (orange shoes, for example) and changes his hairstyle from week to week. I don't believe that they need to worry, because I think he is still working out who he is and trying out different ways of becoming more comfortable with the world around him. I know from my own experience that this process can take time. Steven does volunteer work at a local charity shop and his current obsession is for Triops, small crustaceans that are believed to be the oldest living animal species in the world. He is a very gentle and caring person, and I am proud of him and very hopeful about his future.

Then there is my brother Paul, who is a year younger than Steven and works as a gardener. He has a wide knowledge of plants: when to plant them, where to situate them in the garden, what type of soil each requires, how much sun each plant needs and so on. Whenever I need any advice for my garden, I always know to ask Paul.

The twins are all grown-up, too: Maria, the older by ten minutes, recently passed all her GCSEs with straight As. Like Claire she is a real bookworm and spends a lot of her time reading. Natasha has just given birth to a son, Matthew, making me an uncle for the first time. I have a photo of my nephew on the dresser in my kitchen. Looking at it helps to remind me of the miracles of life and love.

Finally there are my youngest siblings, my sisters Anna-Marie and Shelley. Both are now busy, noisy teenagers. Shelley shares my love of books and especially likes the works of Jane Austen and the Brontë sisters.

Visits to my family are always happy experiences for me. I feel closer to each of them now than I ever could have done growing up. Looking back, I am extremely grateful to them for all the love they have given me and continue to give me. Their support has been a very big reason for any of the success I have had in my life. With every visit, I look forward to our discussions on books and words (and often, inevitably, the Red Hot Chilli Peppers) and to hearing about their experiences and their plans and dreams for the future. I feel truly honoured to be a part of their lives.

I spend most days at home. It is here that I feel most calm, comfortable and secure, because there is order and routine all around me. In the mornings, I always brush my teeth before my shower. I brush each tooth individually and rinse my mouth out afterwards with water. When I wash, I use natural oils – tea tree and jojoba – to help keep my skin clean and soft, as soap is too drying and makes me itch. For breakfast I eat porridge; I love the feel of the texture of the oats on my tongue. I drink cups

of warm tea with skimmed milk, my favourite drink,
throughout the day.

I cook regularly, because it is a tactile experience that
helps me to relax. A recipe is like a mathematical sum
or equation; the product (whether a cake or a casserole)
is the sum of its parts. The ingredients in a recipe have
relationships to each other; if you halve or double one
ingredient, you have to remember to halve or double
the others too. As an example, here is a basic recipe for
a sponge cake that serves six:

6 eggs
340g self-raising flour
340g butter
340g caster sugar

Which can also be written in this way:

6 eggs + 340g self-raising flour + 340g butter +
340g caster sugar = cake (for 6)

To make the cake for three people, instead of six, I
change the product of the sum to: cake (for 3/6); which
is the same as $\frac{1}{2}$, so I halve each ingredient amount in
the sum (3 eggs, 170g flour . . . etc) to arrive at the new
product.

I make a lot of the food that we eat at home using
simple recipes I collect from books or family and
friends. We bake our own bread and make our own

peanut butter for lunchtime sandwiches. Sometimes I make oat milk or yoghurt to snack on. We also make a tasty, low-fat pastry for pies that we fill using apples from the fruit trees in our garden. Neil uses some of the crop to make fresh cider. Neil often helps me in the kitchen and working together on a recipe becomes an opportunity for me to practise my ability to cooperate and communicate effectively as part of a team effort.

The garden also has a large vegetable patch where we grow onions, peas, potatoes, tomatoes, cabbages, lettuces and herbs such as mint, rosemary and sage. I enjoy working in the garden because of the quiet and fresh air and warm sun and because I like to listen to birds singing and watch the insects crawling carefully around the trees and plants. Gardening provides good exercise and is relaxing, requires patience and dedication and helps me feel a greater connection with the world around me.

There is a strong sense of calm and contentment that comes from living in a more self-sufficient way. A soup made from freshly picked homegrown tomatoes is far tastier than anything bought in a shop. My friends really like the personalised birthday cards I make for them from plain cardboard, a pencil and some coloured crayons. Our grocery bills are low, because I plan all our meals weeks in advance and set a budget before we go shopping. Around one third of food grown for consumption in the UK ends up being thrown away, in part because many people buy more than they need.

For a while we shopped each week at our local supermarket, as many people do. However, I would regularly switch off and become anxious and uncommunicative because of the size of the store, the large numbers of shoppers and the amount of stimuli around me. Supermarkets are also often overheated, which is a problem for me because my skin can become itchy and uncomfortable when I feel too warm. Then there are the flickering, fluorescent lights that hurt my eyes. The solution was to go instead to smaller, local shops, which are much more comfortable for me to use, are often less expensive to shop in and support small businesses in our community.

When we go shopping, Neil always drives us because I cannot drive. I have taken my practical test twice in the past, after many lessons, and failed both times. People on the autistic spectrum often need extra experience, practice and concentration when learning to drive. This is because we tend not to have good spatial skills which are necessary when driving a road vehicle. Another difficulty is judging how other road users might behave and understanding that not all drivers obey all the rules all of the time. Fortunately, Neil does not mind doing the driving for both of us.

I have several plans for the future. One is to continue to help charities, such as the National Autistic Society and the National Society for Epilepsy, that are important to me. When I give a talk on behalf of a charity in front of lots of people I sit or stand in such a way as to be able to see Neil in the audience, and I imagine that I'm talking just to him. Then I don't feel so nervous.

I also plan to continue working with scientists and researchers to find out more about my brain and how exactly it works. Following my pi record and the *Brainman* documentary I was inundated with requests to study me from scientists from all over the world. In 2004 I met the world's foremost expert in savant syndrome, Dr Darold Treffert, in Wisconsin in the USA. It was during this meeting that I was told that I matched the condition's diagnostic criteria. Since then, I have contributed regularly to various scientific research projects. Here are two examples of recent studies:

In 2004, Professor Daniel Bor of the Medical Research Council Cognition and Brain Sciences Unit in Cambridge performed an analysis of my digit span – the ability to process sequential numerical information and recall it in the correct order. For each part of the test I was seated in front of a computer screen onto which sequences of numbers were displayed one at a time at a rate of a digit per half-second. After each sequence I was asked to type the numbers into the computer. My recorded digit span was 12 digits, twice the normal range of 5–7 digits. When the computer displayed numbers that had been randomly coloured, to see if they interfered with my synaesthesia, my performance dropped to between 10–11 digits. Professor Bor said that he had never tested anyone before with a digit span above 9 and that my score was extremely rare.

Neil Smith, Professor of Linguistics at University College in London carried out an experiment in the summer of 2005 which looked at how I process certain types of sentence constructions. The sentences all involved what language scientists call 'metalinguistic negation', where the negation works not through the words in the sentence but by how it is expressed. For example, when shown to most people, the sentence 'John isn't tall, he's a giant,' is completely understandable; John is of such height that he can't just be described as tall. However, I only understood this distinction because it was carefully explained to me. The experiment showed that I found such sentences contradictory and difficult to analyse successfully. This is a common problem for individuals on the autistic spectrum, due to the literalness of our thinking and comprehension processes.

There is another way in which I hope that my abilities might help others in the future, by encouraging a wider appreciation of different ways of learning. Visual learning aids can be beneficial to many 'neurotypical' learners, as well as those on the autistic spectrum. For example, using different colours to mark words as noun, verb or adjective can provide a simple and effective introduction to grammar. Similarly, in the online language courses I wrote for my website, new vocabulary is presented with the letters of the words in different sizes, helping to give each word a unique shape. Low-frequency letters such as q, w, x and z are printed small, while medium-frequency letters such as b, c, f and h appear in standard size and high-frequency letters (vowels and consonants such as l, r, s and t) are largest. So the German word *zerquetschen* ('to squash') is introduced as *zerquetschen*, the French word *vieux* ('old') as *vieux* and the Spanish *conozco* ('I know') as *conozco*.

Any aspirations I have for my personal life are really simple: to continue working hard in my relationship with Neil, to carry on practising my communication skills and learning from my mistakes, and taking one day at a time. I also hope to become closer still to my family and friends and that through this book they will know and understand me at least a little better.

I still remember vividly the experience I had as a teenager lying on the floor of my room staring up at the ceiling. I was trying to picture the universe in my head, to have a concrete understanding of what 'everything' was. In my mind I travelled to the edges of existence and looked over them, wondering what I would find. In that instant I felt really unwell and I could feel my heart beating hard inside me, because for the first time I had realised that thought and logic had limits and could only take a person so far. This realisation frightened me and it took me a long time to come to terms with it.

Many people are surprised when they learn that I am a Christian. They imagine that being autistic makes it difficult or impossible to believe in God or explore spiritual issues. It is certainly true that my Asperger's makes it harder for me to have empathy or think abstractly, but it hasn't prevented me from thinking about deeper questions concerning such things as life and death, love and relationships. In fact, many people with autism do find benefits in religious belief or spirituality. Religion's emphasis on ritual, for example, is helpful for individuals with autistic spectrum disorders, who need stability and consistency. In a chapter of her autobiography entitled *Stairway to Heaven: Religion and Belief,* Temple Grandin, an autistic writer and professor of animal science, describes her view of God as an ordering force in the universe. Her religious beliefs stem from her experience of working in the slaughter industry and the feeling she had that there must be something sacred about dying.

Like many people with autism, my religious activity is primarily intellectual rather than social or emotional. When I was at secondary school, I had no interest in religious education and was dismissive of the possibility of a god or that religion could be beneficial to people's lives. This was because God was not something that I could see or hear or feel, and because the religious arguments that I read and heard did not make any sense to me. The turning point came with my discovery of the writings of G.K. Chesterton, an English author and journalist who wrote extensively about his Christian beliefs in the early part the twentieth century.

Chesterton was a remarkable person. At school, his teachers described him as a dreamer and 'not on the same plane as the rest', while as a teenager he set up a debating club with friends, sometimes arguing an idea for hours at a time; he and his brother Cecil once argued for eighteen hours and thirteen minutes. He could quote whole chapters of Dickens and other authors from memory and remembered the plots of all the 10,000 novels he had evaluated as a publisher's reader. His secretaries reported that he would dictate one essay while simultaneously writing another by hand on a different subject. Yet he was always getting lost, so absorbed in his thoughts that he would sometimes have to telegram his wife to help him get back home. He also had a fascination for the everyday things around him, writing in a letter to his wife: 'I do not think there is anyone who takes quite such a fierce pleasure in things, being themselves, as I do. The startling wetness of water excites and intoxicates me. The fieriness of fire, the steeliness of steel, the unutterable muddiness of mud.' It's possible that Chesterton was on the higher-functioning end of the autistic spectrum himself; certainly I have always felt close to him from reading about his experiences and ideas.

Reading Chesterton as a teenager helped me to arrive at an intellectual understanding of God and Christianity. The concept of the Trinity, of God as composed of a living and loving relationship, was something that I could picture in my head and that made sense to me. I was also fascinated by the idea of the Incarnation, of God revealing Himself to the world in tangible, human form as Jesus Christ. Even so, it was not until I was twenty-three that I decided to participate in a course at a local church, aimed at teaching the basics of Christianity in weekly, social meetings. Each week I would come to the meeting and exhaust my fellow group members by asking question after question. I wasn't interested in praying for guidance or listening to the experiences of others, but in getting answers to my questions. Fortunately, Chesterton answered each of them for me in his books. At Christmas 2002 I became a Christian.

My autism can sometimes make it difficult for me to understand how other people might think or feel in any given situation. For this reason, my moral values are based more on ideas that are logical, make sense to me and that I have thought through carefully, than on the ability to 'walk in another person's shoes'. I know to treat each person I meet with kindness and respect, because I believe that each person is unique and created in God's image.

I do not often attend church, because I can become uncomfortable with having lots of people sitting and standing around me. However, on the few occasions when I have been inside a church I have found the experience very interesting and affecting. The architecture is often complex and beautiful and I really like having lots of space above my head as I look up at the high ceilings. As in childhood, I enjoy listening to hymns being sung. Music definitely helps me to experience feelings that can be described as religious, such as of unity and transcendence. My favourite song is 'Ave Maria'. Whenever I hear it, I feel completely wrapped up inside the flow of the music.

Some of my favourite stories are from the Bible, such as the story of David and Goliath. Many of them use symbolic and picturesque language that I can visualise and that helps me to understand the narratives. There are many beautiful and inspiring passages in the Bible, but one I especially like is the following from 1 Corinthians: 'Love is patient, love is kind. Love is not envious, jealous or boastful. It is not arrogant or rude. Love does not insist on its own ways. It is not irritable or resentful. It does not rejoice at wrong and wrongdoing, but rejoices in right and truth. Love bears all things, believes all things, hopes all things, endures all things. Love never ends. So faith, hope and love abide these three. But the greatest of these is love.'

Everyone is said to have a perfect moment once in a while, an experience of complete peace and connection, like looking out from the top of the Eiffel Tower or watching a falling star high in the night sky. I do not have many such moments, but Neil says that is okay because being rare is what makes them so special. My most recent came one weekend last summer at home – they often happen to me while I am at home – after a meal I had cooked and eaten with Neil. We were sitting together in the living room, feeling full and happy. All of a sudden I experienced a kind of self-forgetting and in that brief, shining moment all my anxiety and awkwardness seemed to disappear. I turned to Neil and asked him if he had felt the same sensation and he said he had.

I imagine these moments as fragments or splinters scattered across a lifetime. If a person could somehow collect them all up and stick them together he would have a perfect hour or even a perfect day. And I think in that hour or day he would be closer to the mystery of what it is to be human. It would be like having a glimpse of heaven.